the new
complete
tourist
guide

Siena

The Town
The Monuments
The Museums
The Palio
The Cooking

TEMPO LIBERO

by sillabe

Sienese 8 Itineraries

© 2008 **sillabe** s.r.l.
Livorno
www.sillabe.it
info@sillabe.it
managing editor:
Maddalena Paola Winspeare
texts: *Antonella Capitanio*
Sienese cooking texts:
Ethel Santacroce
graphic design:
Laura Belforte
lay-out: *Fabrizio Bagatti*
editing: *Giulia Bastianelli*
translation:
Catherine Burnett

Authorized by the
"Consorzio per la Tutela del
Palio di Siena"
ISBN 978-88-8347-417-0

(*) panoramic view
(🍴) additional material
(✋) not to be missed!
Museums… in italics

Reproduction rights: *Archivio Opera della Metropolitana; Archivio di Stato di Siena; Pinacoteca Nazionale di Siena; Foto Lensini, Siena; Archivio sillabe: foto B. Bruchi, C. Cascioli, L. Belforte*

The Publisher is at the disposal of the the copyright holders of images from unidentified sources.

INTRODUCTION

OTHER VIEWS
"Siena looks over me
always looks over me
from its far high ground
or from that of memories…"
MARIO LUZI, *Simone Martini's terrestrial and celestial journey* (1994)

The verses with which the Tuscan poet imagines what the great fourteenth-century Sienese painter would have thought of the town as he found himself far away in Avignon magnificently summarises a sensation that anyone arriving in Siena can feel: the town, spread out over its hills with its soaring municipal tower, really seems to be looking over people as they arrive. This guide aims to turn that glimpse around, urging visitors to take a look at the town as a whole in order to capture the civic identity which makes it unique – practically the biggest "urban museum" of the European Middle Ages.

"We arrive in the city of Siena
positioned on a beautiful plain
Of grace and fine customs it is rich,
of charming women and courteous men,
and the air is sweet, clear and serene.
This city as someone told me,
when the elders of Brenno settled here
and the Romans were captured and killed,
grew fast; and there are others
that say, when the good Carlo Martello
passed through, his elders founded the city.
I saw its Campo, which is very beautiful,
and I saw Fonte Branda and Camollia
and the hospital, which everybody still talks about.
I saw the church of Santa Maria
with its marble inlays and, when these sights
had been seen,
we made our way towards Arezzo."

FAZIO DEGLI UBERTI, *Il Dittamondo*, (1346–1369) III, chap. VIII, vv. 68–84

Going up towards the Cathedral

The She-Wolf, a symbol of Siena

Describing one of his imaginary allegorical voyages in Europe and Africa Farinata's great-grandson, who was immortalised by Dante, paints a wonderful picture of how people perceived the town of Siena in the fourteenth century. He touches upon its historical roots and sheds light upon places which are still important today – the Piazza del Campo, the large public buildings, the Hospital of Santa Maria della Scala and the Cathedral with its extraordinary series of external sculptures. In short, all the places which continue to embody the town's image.

Siena still has the same urban system which has defined its identity through the ages. The town's position on a group of hills has allowed it to avoid being integrated into the vast array of constructions outside the walls leaving the nucleus of the old town centre intact. In the Middle Ages this area was a hub for the economic, political and cultural power which generated a real "Sienese civilisation". This was a small victory over fate which then saw it defeated and subjugated to its rival Florence.

The origins of the settlement are said to be linked to those of Rome with its foundation attributed to Remus' twin sons Aschio and Senio (to whom the town owes its name) when they took flight after their father's murder. The medieval chronicler Giovanni Villani, on the other hand, ascribes the town's origins to the "old and infirm" Senones that were left by the wayside when the Gallic people occupied Rome but the motive for mockery on the part of the Florentine historian is obvious in a very Tuscan gibe towards a rival

Pintoricchio, *Enea Silvio Piccolomini presents Eleanor of Aragon to Frederick III at Porta Camollia* (detail), 1505–1507, fresco. Cathedral. Piccolomini Library

town. The most likely story is that the name derived from the Etruscan family Saina who used to dominate the area, as Pliny the Elder refers to Siena as an Etruscan colony in the first century AD. The location, which is not particularly favourable, appears to be motivated by the presence in the valleys of natural springs, a result of the tuffaceous nature of the overlying hills on marly layers. The network of ancient public sources also provides clear evidence of how much of a cornerstone to the city they were, representing, in fact, one of its most characteristic phenomena. A monumental linchpin is the Fonte Gaia, a Renaissance element of the medieval Piazza del Campo supplied,

Porta Tufi
Inside the "Bottini"

however, by an older water system made up of 25 kilometres of tunnels called BOTTINI (open to visitors upon reservation) which carried water to over 50 fountains from the Middle Ages onwards, most of which were situated near the city gates. The Pescaia fountain outside the Porta Camollia was built to supply water to the fish tanks which were used to supply provisions to the town. There were two in the area around Porta Ovile – one outside the gate which was named after it and one inside the gate which was known as the New Fountain. The most famous Fountain was at Porta Branda and bore the same name as the gate but all of them had the same typical form with a large portico opened out by arches.

Other more important gates around the city walls include Porta Romana, Porta Pispini, Porta Tufi, Porta San Marco and Porta Laterina, and all of them were originally decorated with frescoed shrines which are not all very well

Detail of the fresco on the outer gate of
Porta Camollia

Sano di Pietro, *San Pietro Alessandrino between
Blessed Andrea Gallerani and Blessed Ambrogio
Sansedoni* (detail), 1446. Palazzo Pubblico,
Room of the She-Wolves

preserved. Unlike most walled cities, which usually had an extremely
limited number of entrances, Siena stood out because of its multiple
gates, even private ones, a sign of its prevalent particularism.

The walls are the result of a series of consecutive enlargements which,
after the first nucleus of Castelvecchio and the Cathedral, went on to include first the eastern area outlined by Via Francigena, and then the south-
ern area. This was an urban development with an obvious link to the road
axes which were in all likelihood also responsible, as we will discover, for
the construction of an entrance way to the cathedral church positioned
under the apsidal area.

OTHER VIEWS

"It is a very irregular town, built upon the ridge of a hill, along
which the best streets lie; the other streets run down the two sides,
in different directions, some of them turning back, and coming
half-way up again."

Montaigne, *The Diary of Montaigne's Journey to Italy through Switzerland and Ger-
many* (1580–1581)

*Montaigne's words evoke the effort required to get around Siena if one does not
take the differences in level into consideration but the character of the city is also
created by the narrow and steep lanes which reward visitors with evocative views
and unexpected openings onto breathtaking panoramas.*

The following pages of this guide suggest itineraries that are based on a
central circuit "in the heart of the city", Itinerary **0**. This itinerary is essential in order to gain a feel for the place and is organised into seven different
ways of reaching that objective.

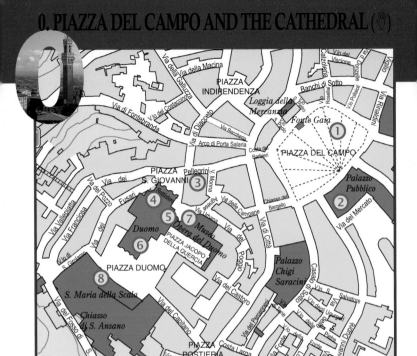

OTHER VIEWS

"We went off, betimes next morning, to see the Cathedral, which is wonderfully picturesque inside and out, especially the latter – also the market place, or great Piazza, which is a large square, with a great broken-nosed fountain in it: some quaint Gothic houses: and a high square brick tower; outside the top of which – a curious feature in such views in Italy – hangs an enormous bell. It is like a bit of Venice, without the water."

CHARLES DICKENS, *Pictures from Italy* (1846)

The English writer's impressions leave the reader somewhat perplexed for the rather belittling tone he uses to dismiss the Piazza del Campo – at the time it was the site of a travelling market and Jacopo della Quercia's Fonte Gaia had not yet been substituted with the copy by Tito Sarrocchi (1868) – but the extraordinary comparison to a "Venice without water" is perhaps the most beautiful image ever evoked about this enchanting place, next to which even the "shell of a time past" suggested by Nathaniel Hawthorne (1883) seems banal.

The urban breadth of this great ansate and sloping space, with the Palazzo Pubblico set along the lower side in a non dominating yet important position, really represents the only possible similarity with the basin of St. Mark in front of the Palazzo Ducale in Venice.

◇
1 Piazza del Campo

The area which now appears to be in the heart of the city actually lies outside the walls of the early Middle Ages and it was only built, like the Palazzo Pubblico, in the era of the Council of Nine, in power between 1287 and 1355.

The idea for the paving covering the square can be traced back to 1347. It is made up of tiles in a herringbone pattern, divided into nine sections by white stone stripes which fan out from the lower area. The design enhances the Palazzo Pubblico as a focal point, with the Fonte Gaia sitting opposite on higher ground. This was a Renaissance work of art by **Jacopo della Quercia** (1409–1419), whose original sculptures – substituted by the above mentioned copies by **Tito Sarrocchi** – can be found in the museum complex of Santa Maria della Scala.

The Fountain was commissioned in 1408 to **Jacopo della Quercia**, the greatest Sienese sculptor of all time and it was completed before the end of 1419. The fluid plasticity of form can still be sensed in the relief with the *Madonna and Child* and in the statue depicting *Acca Larentia with Romulus and Remus*, while the relief with the *Expulsion of Adam and Eve from Paradise* precedes the masterpiece of the same subject which the artist made for the gate of St. Petronius in Bologna.

Among the buildings around the square some stand out more than others:

  a. Palazzo Chigi Zondadari sits on the corner of Via Rinaldi and owes it current appearance to an eighteenth-century renovation. Evidence of this can be seen inside in the leather linings covering entire walls, but these originate from the unification of a group of older houses and towers.

  b. Palazzo Sansedoni sits next door and it too was renovated at the beginning

Fonte Gaia

Jacopo della Quercia, *Rhea Silvia*, 1408–1419. Santa Maria della Scala

of the eighteenth century. During this renovation buildings from the thirteenth century which had been worked on in 1339 by **Agostino di Giovanni** were joined together. Inside the building – currently the premises of the Monte dei Paschi Foundation – there is a spectacular late baroque chapel characterised by supple decorative ornamentation by **Massimiliano Soldani Benzi** and the **Mazzuoli** family.

c. Between the San Paolo and San Pietro alleyways the rear façade of the LOGGIA DELLA MERCANZIA can be seen exactly as **Ferdinando Fuga** originally intended in 1763.

d. Moving on we can see the CASE DE METZ, houses with the vestiges of gothic windows.

e. Beyond the Costarella dei Barbari we can see the sixteenth-century PALAZZO D'ELCI, characterised by the boundary battlements.

◇
2 PALAZZO PUBBLICO

Building work began in 1297 and the middle part with three floors was completed around 1308–1310. In the following decades work proceeded on the sides (which remained, however, as a single floor until the seventeenth century) and in 1348 work on the TOWER came to an end, known thereafter as DEL MANGIA after the name of the first bell-ringer. The architect behind the project remains unknown but according to documentary sources "**Maestro Giovanni**", an illuminator and calligrapher features among the people who oversaw the building work. For the tower, however, the names of two brothers from Perugia called **Minuccio** and **Francesco di Rinaldo** are registered along with "Magistro Filippo pictori", thought to be **Lippo Memmi** – brother-in-law and co-worker of **Simone Martini** – who could have provided the

design or most probably a painting of the construction. Although we cannot be sure of these assertions, the technical skills of the various people supposed to be involved highlight the fundamental coherence that typified artistic traditions at the time.

The structure is notable for its curved façade which underlines its connection with the square opposite. The large copper disc painted with the monogram of Christ enclosed in a shining sun is a symbol of St. Bernardine and can be traced back to 1425. The sermons the Saint preached in front of the building were held at around the same time according to the images depicted in a painting by **Sano di Pietro,** now in the Museo dell'Opera del Duomo, providing evidence of the original appearance of the CHAPEL OF PIAZZA DEL CAMPO. The loggia sits to the left, right against the façade and in line with the tower above. It was built from a design by **Domenico d'Agostino** from 1352 onwards as a votive offering after the disastrous plague of 1348 but it was reworked into a Renaissance style by **Antonio Federighi** (1463–1468).

In 1560, a year after the definitive annexation of Siena to the Florentine state, the Medici coat of arms was placed on the façade while the addition of two extra floors on either side of the central structure was attributable to a project by the architect **Carlo Fontana**, who also included other internal areas in the design (1680–1681). At the end of the nineteenth century the building was restored to a neo-medieval form and the monumental salons were opened to visitors but the Civic Museum was not created until the 1930s.

Entering the building through the right gateway the SALA DELLE LUPE (ROOM OF THE SHE-WOLVES) is on the ground floor. It was named after two spouts for draining rain water attributed to **Giovanni Pisano**, placed there after the severe consumption in the town and substituted on the outside of the building by copies. There is also a fresco by **Sano di Pietro** in the room featuring the Sienese Saints *Pietro Alessandrino*, *Ambrogio Sansedoni* and *Andrea Gallerani*. This area, however, is not part of the normal visitors' itinerary as the tourist entrance is through the left gateway near the Cappella di Piazza opening onto the COURTYARD OF THE PODESTÀ and from there people can climb the four hundred steps to the top of the Torre del Mangia and have their exertion rewarded with a spectacular panorama. (*PANORAMIC VIEW)

Sano di Pietro, *St. Bernardine's Sermon in Piazza del Campo*, 1444–1450. Museo dell'Opera del Duomo
The Chapel of Piazza del Campo
One of the She-Wolves at the top of the Torre del Mangia

At the back of the courtyard there is also an entrance to the TEATRO COMMUNALE DEI RINNOVATI. This was originally the Room of the Consiglio Maggiore della Repubblica (General Council of the Republic), built at the beginning of the fourteenth century at the back of Palazzo Pubblico. From 1560 onwards it became the permanent venue for theatre productions for the Medici family after Cosimo visited the city for the first time on the 26th of January of the same year. The theatre went through a series of renovations which were initially overseen by **Bartolomeo Neroni** known as **Riccio**, then **Carlo Fontana** probably in 1667 and then the famous theatre architect **Antonio Galli Bibiena** between 1751 and 1753. The room

Inside the Torre del Mangia
View from the Courtyard of the Podestà

owes its current appearance to a project by the architect **Agostino Fantastici** which was carried out in the 1830s.

The entrance to the Palazzo is on the right side of the Courtyard where visitors can also gain access to the MAGAZZINI DEL SALE (STOREROOMS OF SALT) below, an evocative space which currently houses temporary exhibitions. The itinerary taken by visitors, on the other hand, leads to the first floor and even the stairwell holds works of great historical-artistic interest like, for example, the bell made in 1109 by **Maestro Alberto**.

Once the visitor reaches the upper, noble floor there is a picture gallery containing noteworthy sinopia of frescoes for the Chapel of Piazza del Campo done by **Sodoma** (1537–1539). There is no lack, however, of other rare evidence of the city's history like, for example, the seventeenth-century *Procession in Piazza del Duomo* by **Agostino Marcucci** and a noteworthy collection of seals, coins and medals (only some of which are on display). This gallery marks the beginning of the visitor's route through the historical rooms starting with the most recent, the SALA DEL RISORGIMENTO, with the celebration of Vittorio Emanuele II's victorious mission to unify Italy entrusted to **Amos Cassioli**, **Cesare Maccari** and **Pietro Aldi**, all pupils of **Luigi Mussini**, master of the Sienese Academy. This room was completed between 1886 and 1888 and inaugurated in 1890. It has retained both the coeval sculptures of **Enea Becheroni**, **Emilio Gallori**, **Tito Sarrocchi** and others, and the uniform worn by the king in the battle of San Martino. This battle was a fundamental episode

Room of the Risorgimento

of the second War of Independence and is commemorated here in a painting by Cassioli given to Mussini by Vittorio Emanuele to thank him for the portrait he painted of the king.

The next room is the SALA DI BALIA (ROOM OF AUTHORITY), the place where the old magistracy would act in secret and quickly in unusual emergency situations. The vaults were frescoed by **Martino di Bartolomeo** between 1407 and 1408 and at the same time **Spinello Aretino** and his son **Parri Spinelli** were working on the walls. The artists covered them in full scenes and the most original among them in terms of subject was certainly the one portraying the *Naval Battle of Punta San Salvatore*. The ANTICAMERA DEL CONCISTORO (ANTECHAMBER OF THE CONSISTORY) comes next and holds various works of art including a *Madonna and Child* by **Matteo di Giovanni** and a notable fifteenth-century doorway attributed to **Rossellino**. The doorway leads to the SALA DEL CONCISTORO (HALL OF THE CONSISTORY) or rather the room where the government of the old Republic used to meet and it is for this reason that it is decorated with a cycle of paintings depicting the *Public Virtues* and their exemplary use in classic antiquity. The paintings were done by **Domenico Beccafumi** between 1529 and 1535 using a chromatic freshness which rendered complex compositions and obsolete subjects visually brilliant, like in *The Sacrifice of Codros, King of Athens* or *The Reconciliation of Lepidus and Flaccus*. The *Judgement of Salomon* (1680 ca) by **Luca Giordano** sits above the door.

Simone Martini, *Maestà*, fresco (whole and detail)

Simone Martini, *Guidoriccio da Fogliano*, fresco

Duccio di Buoninsegna (?), *Capture of a castle* (1314), fresco

Retracing your steps, going to the right through the Vestibule there is a *She-Wolf*, a symbol of the town made by the goldsmith and sculptor **Giovanni di Turino** (1429–1430). This was once on an external column of Palazzo Pubblico as a symbol of the old subdivision of the city into thirds, just as the other two thirds had their symbols in Piazza Tolomei and Piazza Postierla. The same symbol can be found on the small plaque by the same artist in the room's display cabinet, which also brings together various other precious relics of civic identity.

The vestibule faces the building's original flight of stairs and leads to the splendid Sala del Mappamondo (Room of the Planisphere) which was named after the lost work by **Ambrogio Lorenzetti**. This is the biggest room in the Palazzo and meetings of the Consiglio Generale della Repubblica originally used to take place here. The far wall is dominated by the *Maestà* by **Simone Martini** who started painting the work in 1312 and completed it in June 1315 but worked on it again in 1321.

The *Madonna enthroned under a bald-achin surrounded by angels and saints* is a sumptuous depiction of a celestial court and highlights Martini's refined preciosity in artistic technique as he enriched the fresco with widespread use of vellum, glass, gold leaf and even a large, convex rock crystal practically in the centre of the composition to physically become the clasp on the Virgin's cloak. This work is obviously dependent on the place in which it is positioned and has come to signify more than just a depiction of a religious subject. It presents the Madonna as a guarantor of the good government of the city almost as if she were in direct contact with its governors through the patron saints Ansanus, Savinus, Crescentius and Victor. The saints intercede with her and in fact the Virgin responds: *"Diletti mei ponete nelle menti / che li devoti vostri preghi onesti / come vorrete voi farò co[n]tenti / ma se i potenti ai debili fien molesti / gravando loro o con vergogne o danni / le vostre oration non son per questi / né per qualunque la mia terra inganni"* (*"My dearest remember / that your honest prayers / I will grant as you wish / but if those in power take advantage of the weak / oppressing them with destruction or harm / your prayers will not be heard / nor those of anybody who deceives my land."*). *This affirmation is supported by the cartouche in Baby Jesus' hand which holds the first words of the Book of Knowledge,* "Diligite Iustitiam qui iudicatis terram" (*"Choose Justice you who judge the land"*), and the inscription which runs along the step of the throne: *"Li angelichi fiorecti, rose e gigli, / onde s'adorna lo celeste prato, / non mi dilettan più che i buon' consigli. / Ma talor veggio chi per proprio stato / disprezza me e la mie tera inganna, / e quando parla peggio è più lodato. / Guardi ciascun cui questo dir conda[n]na"* (*Roses and lilies, angelic flowers, / which decorate the celestial garden, / good advice no longer interests me. / But sometimes I see that, those who by nature / disregard me and deceive my land / are praised even more when they speak badly. / Beware thee who these words condemn."*). Throughout the room scenes were frescoed with the various Sienese saints as if to reiterate the theme of protection and control over the conduct of the governors. On the wall opposite the window **Sano di Pietro** completed a *St. Bernardine* in 1450, the very year of his canonisation. **Vecchietta** did *St. Catherine* in 1460, **Sodoma** depicted the founder of the Olivetans *Blessed Bernardo Tolomei* around 1530 and he had already painted *St. Victor* and *St. Ansanus* on the wall opposite

the *Maestà* in 1529. There is, however, a much more famous painting hanging over the two saints, the so-called *Guidoriccio da Fogliano*. This depicts a monumental character on horseback dominating a landscape dotted with military settlements which **Simone Martini** started painting in 1328, although the discovery of a painting underneath with the same subject featuring two people and a castle has given rise to a diatribe on the true identification of the much documented work.

From here visitors pass into the SALA DEI NOVE (ROOM OF THE NINE) whose name reflects its original purpose, celebrating the people who commissioned the spectacular cycle of frescoes around its walls. The *Allegories* and the *Effects of Good and Bad Government* are the first, rare examples of painting with civic subjects and were completed in 1337 by **Ambrogio Lorenzetti**. The precarious state of conservation of the part about "bad government" highlights, among other things, the conceptual contrast with the good side in an effective summary of what we would recognise today as a governmental programme. The painting progresses along the walls and is subdivided into four large sections reaching the height of excellence in the depiction of the city and the surrounding area which are full of life thanks to the good government. In the

Ambrogio Lorenzetti, *The effects of Good Government in the city and in the countryside, Allegory of Bad Government, Allegory of Good Government*, frescoes

allegorical interpretation the good government appears as an old wise man assisted by the cardinal virtues, side by side with Peace and Magnanimity while Justice assisted by Wisdom is positioned separately but on the same plane in order to emphasise the necessary independence between them.

In the following room, known as the room of the PILLARS, there are paintings, illuminated manuscripts, furnishings and a stained glass window depicting *St. Michael* from a design by **Duccio di Buoninsegna**.

Back in the Sala del Mappamondo visitors can pass through the antechapel frescoed in 1415 by **Taddeo di Bartolo** with images of the virtues required in the exertion of power – Justice, Magnanimity, Fortitude, Prudence and Religion – and figures such as Cato or Mucius Scaevola who made ancient Rome great thanks to these qualities. A map of ancient Rome is depicted on the arch over the entrance to the Sala del Mappamondo and on the wall opposite there is a painting of customarily gigantic proportions of St. Christopher. According to legend St. Christopher carried Christ over his shoulders and therefore the weight of the whole world. His presence inside the Palazzo Pubblico cannot be explained by his usual role as the patron saint of travellers but rather for his being one of the fourteen "auxiliary saints" invoked in case of unusual

Domenico di Niccolò dei Cori, *The Virgin Mary entrusts Siena to Podestà*

Piazza del Mercato and the back of Palazzo Pubblico with the Loggia

illnesses or calamities. This was a common occurrence during the fourteenth century and saw Christopher rise to protector against the plague, which had a disastrous effect on Siena around the middle of the century when almost two thirds of the population died.

The CHAPEL is separated from the rest of the room by a gate which can be traced back to 1437. It is frescoed with *Stories of the Virgin*, again by **Taddeo di Bartolo**, and is especially significant for its original furnishings. The choir was inlaid between 1415 and 1428 by **Domenico di Niccolò** who became known as "dei Cori" (of the Choirs) after its completion. The rare torch holder hanging from the ceiling in polychrome and gilded wood can also be ascribed to Domenico di Niccolò while there is an organ by **Giovanni d'Antonio Piffaro** on the right side of the altar which is just as rare and can be dated to around 1520.

The altar and the painting on wood by Sodoma depicting *The Sacred family of St. Leonard* (1530 ca) were not destined for this room, although they were destined for the Cathedral. They were moved here at the end of the seventeenth century. Precious objects linked to sacred rituals are kept in two display cabinets in the antechapel and among them there is another rare object, the *Rosa d'oro* (*Golden Rose*). This was a token of appreciation awarded annually by Popes to people who had distinguished themselves in the defence of the Church and in 1458 it was given by Pius II Piccolomini to his city of origin. Pius II had it made by the Florentine **Simone di Giovanni di Giovanni Ghini,** the most well-known goldsmith working in Rome for the papal court in the fifteenth century. The visitor's route proceeds up a great flight of stairs and half way up there is a GIPSOTECA (GALLERY OF PLASTER CASTS) which houses casts made over a century ago of some important works of Sienese sculpture to allow an overview of them all together. The famous *Funerary monument of Ilaria del Carretto* by **Jacopo della Quercia** at Lucca can be seen among the casts. You can then go up to the wonderful LOGGIA which looks over the PIAZZA DEL MERCATO on one side and provides a spectacular panorama over the south of the city. (*PANORAMIC VIEW)

Upon leaving Palazzo Pubblico you can cross the Piazza del Campo diagonally to walk up to the opposite corner and pass through Costarella dei Barbieri. Proceeding along Via dei Pellegrini – a name which indicates the fact the pilgrims took this very path when they came through Siena on their way to Rome during the Middle Ages – the PALAZZO DEL MAGNIFICO is on the left.

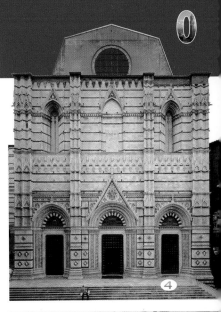

◇
3 PALAZZO DEL MAGNIFICO

This was built in 1508 from a design by **Giacomo Cozzarelli** for Pandolfo Petrucci, a Lord of the city known as "il Magnifico" (the Magnificent). The internal decoration was entrusted to **Signorelli**, **Genga** and **Pintoricchio** and it included an extraordinary ceiling inspired by the golden vault of the *Domus Aurea* which had just been rediscovered in Rome. The frescoes were detached in the nineteenth century so some are now at the Metropolitan Museum in New York and some are at the National Gallery in London while the only ones left at the National Art Gallery (Pinacoteca Nazionale) in Siena are the *Flight of Aeneas from Troy* and *The son of Fabius Maximus frees the prisoners from Hannibal*, both by **Girolamo Genga**.

You then come to Piazza San Giovanni, dominated by the Baptistery which bears the same name.

◇
4 BAPTISTERY

The Baptistery is set in the area underneath the apsidal part of the Cathedral. Building work started in 1316 under the supervision of Camaino di Crescentino. Work on the incomplete façade began in 1355 under Domenico d'Agostino and it is characterised by the presence of numerous gothic elements like the arched gateways bordered by spiral columns, the series of little pensile cuspidal arches, the niches and the large windows crowned by spires just like the central gateway. The marble floor of the parvis on

Baptistery, details of the façade

Inside the Baptistery

Donatello, *Herod's Banquet*, panel from the
Baptismal Font

the other hand, has fifteenth-century ornamentation with three scenes linked to the rite of Baptism. One of them is ascribed to **Bartolomeo di Mariano** and the other two are attributed to **Antonio Federighi**. The inside also adds to the gothic nature of the Baptistery with fifteenth-century ornamentation such as the frescoes by **Michele di Matteo**, **Benvenuto di Giovanni**, **Pietro degli Orioli** and **Lorenzo di Pietro** known as **Vecchietta**. Vecchietta's *Articles of the Creed* on the vaulting

near the altars stand out for their high quality. Another cardinal work and the most well-known in this setting is the Baptismal Font which can also be traced back to the fifteenth century. The most eminent sculptors of the time worked on the Font including **Donatello**, **Ghiberti** and **Jacopo della Quercia**, assisted by the equally talented **Turino di Sano**, **Giovanni di Turino** and **Goro di ser Neroccio**. It is a marble structure with a large ciborium rising up from the hexagonal basin characterised by the *Scenes from the life of the Baptist* in gilded bronze which are separated at the edges by figures of the *Virtues* in the same material. Of all the Font's components the relief of *Herod's Banquet* by **Donatello** provides an admirable example of Renaissance perspective techniques. In contrast, there is a painting on the high altar of the *Baptism of Christ* by **Alessandro Franchi** who, in 1907 at almost seventy years old, was a faithful interpreter of nineteenth-century purist principals while the right-hand altar holds a neo gothic triptych by **Giuseppe Catani Chiti**.

Upon leaving the Baptistery and climbing the adjacent flight of steps, designed in 1451 by **Giovanni Sabatelli**, you come out along the right side of the Cathedral into Piazza del Duomo. This route is almost an evocation of the sacred path up to the acropolis passing under the great archway which creates a perfect entrance way, but in actual fact it is part of the remains of the construction work on the New Cathedral (1339–1355). This was a grandiose structure designed by **Lando di Pietro** which would have reduced the existing building to a simple transept, as seen by the spectacular façade. Like the archway, the façade was done by **Giovanni d'Agostino**, sitting isolated on the left with its enormous gothic windows open to the sky.

◇
5 Crypt

The steps actually hold a symbol of the popular devotion to St. Catherine as one of them is marked by a cross where, as tradition has it, the Saint once fell over after being pushing by the devil. As you go up the steps the entrance to one of the most intriguing places in the Cathedral is on the right and its charm is heightened by the fact it has only recently been discovered. The restoration work on the rooms under the choir of the Cathedral in 2001 actually brought to light a fascinating area entirely covered in frescoes which provides significant evidence of both the use of painting incorporated into architecture and the Sienese pictorial culture of the second half of the thir-

⑤

teenth century. It has also allowed us to form a clearer idea of the artistic characteristics of people such as **Guido da Siena**, **Dietisalvi di Speme**, **Guido di Graziano** and **Rinaldo da Siena**.

The fact that this area has been kept in darkness and has not been tampered with over time means we can now behold paintings with particularly bright colours covering all the surfaces from the walls to the pillars, columns, capitals and all the other architectural framework. The stories narrated are *Scenes from the Old and New Testaments* including, in the case of the latter Testament, episodes from the Apocrypha like the one relating to the *Flight from Egypt* with the palm bending its branches towards Baby Jesus and the Virgin Mary to allow them to pick dates.

The purpose of this area is disputed, but the fact that it is positioned along the hill which brought pilgrims into the city from Via Francigena to the Cathedral is certainly significant.

Inside the Crypt
Gateway of the New Cathedral

OTHER VIEWS

"Here I have sat a while every morning for a week, like a philosophic convalescent, watching the florid facade of the cathedral glitter against the deep blue sky. It has been lavishly restored of late years and the fresh white marble of the densely clustered pinnacles and statues and beasts and flowers flashes in the sunshine like a mosaic of jewels.

There is more of this goldsmith's work in stone than I can remember or describe; it is piled over three great doors with immense margins of exquisite decorative sculpture – still in the ancient cream – coloured marble – and beneath three sharp pediments embossed with images relieved against red marble and tipped with golden mosaics. It is in the highest degree fantastic and luxuriant – it is on the whole very

lovely. As a triumph of the many-hued it prepares you for the interior, where the same parti-coloured splendour is endlessly at play – a confident complication of harmonies and contrasts and of the minor structural refinements and braveries. The internal surface is mainly wrought in alternate course of black and white marble; but as the latter has been dimmed by the centuries to a fine mild brown the place is all a concert of relieved and dispersed glooms."

HENRY JAMES, *Italian Hours* (1873-1909)

James' subtle sensibility and the exceptional nature of his writing impress once again in this description of the Duomo of Siena as he succeeds in making us believe we are actually there. His comments on the restorations which were taking place at practically the same time as his repeated visits are also of an admirable standard. He obviously does not entirely approve of the restorations but appreciates them nonetheless for the distinctive visual beauty given to the whole. The more surprising comment, however, is the definition of the façade as a "work of goldsmithery in stone" which precedes all the studies on the fundamental role of art-guide played by the Sienese goldsmiths towards the end of the thirteenth century and the beginning of the following century when the sculptures on this part of the building were being completed.

Room of the Central Gatewy. Museo dell'Opera del Duomo.
Inside the Cathedral with a view of the floor

◇
6 CATHEDRAL

The Cathedral is dedicated to Our Lady of the Assumption and was built from around the middle of the twelfth century onwards on the site of an older church which was itself, in the customary continuity of worship based on the perception of a place being sacred, a substitute for a roman temple dedicated to Minerva. The structure was completed in 1215 but the dome was not finished until the middle of the century when **Nicola de Apulia**, the sculptor better known as **Nicola Pisano**, was in the city. This artist's surname, de Apulia, is indicative of where he came from and explains the origins of his classic culture, typical of the Puglia region at the time of King Frederick. The "gallery of statues" design of the façade, on the other hand, was down to his son **Giovanni** who worked on it between 1285 and 1296. For reasons of conservation the original pieces are now in the Museo dell'Opera and have been substituted by copies to preserve the façade's visual coherence. One original feature is the architrave

The Piccolomini Library

of the central gateway with the *Stories of Joachim and Anne* by **Tino di Camaino** while the tympana of the three gates hold busts of *Blessed Giovanni Colombini*, *Ambrogio Sansedoni* and *Andrea Gallerani* by **Tommaso Redi** which were added in the seventeenth century. The upper part of the façade was completed after 1376 by **Giovanni di Cecco** and imitates that of Orvieto Cathedral, although the mosaics which decorate the three spires can be traced back to 1877 and were made from cartoons by **Luigi Mussini** and **Alessandro Franchi**. The spires thus provide extremely interesting evidence of the re-emergence of this ancient technique during the nineteenth-century revival. The pavement of the parvis is decorated with marble inlays depicting the priesthood ordination ceremonies, even though these are only copies of the fifteenth-century originals by **Nastagio di Gaspare**. The church is characterised by the two colours of the horizontal white and

Giovanni Paciarelli, *Plan of the Cathedral floor*, 1884. Siena, Museo dell'Opera

black stripes which are present throughout the architectural structure except on the vaults. As visitors enter the building three naves open out under round arches supported by clustered pillars. The work of art which stands out from the others is the paving. It cannot be appreciated as a whole unless flight inside the Cathedral were to become possible, so in reality it was conceived *ad maiorem gloriam dei* (*to the greater glory of God*). Furthermore, conservation problems have rightly led to the frequented parts of the floor being kept under panels which hide it from view, except at certain times of the year. To form a complete picture, visitors must look at the nineteenth century drawings in the Museo dell'Opera where the underlying fourteenth-century original parts of the floor are also kept.

These original parts depict symbols of the city and are composed using a mosaic technique. The Cathedral contains some examples of graffito, although the absolutely magnificent larger area was done using an inlay technique which, according to the designer and the time it was conceived, favoured either a graphic or a pictorial effect.

The complex iconographic design sets out an ideal path to the altar and hence to Christ, through episodes of classic, Hebrew and evangelical history. The creators of the designs were the great leaders of Sienese art such as **Sassetta**, **Francesco di Giorgio Martini**, **Pintoricchio** and **Beccafumi**. Beccafumi may have created the most magnificent images in the Cathedral between 1519 and 1524 in the upper

The Chapel of St. John the Baptist

half of the hexagon under the dome with the *Stories of Elijah and Ahab*. The most substantial part of the project was worked on between 1369 and 1562. The documentary evidence of the later integration work around the end of the nineteenth century is also very interesting as it was based on the drawings by **Luigi Mussini** and **Alessandro Franchi**. As regards the rest of the ornamentation the most famous paintings originally intended for the interior of the building like the *Maestà* by **Duccio di Buoninsegna**, the *Annunciation* by **Simone Martini** and the *Nativity* by **Pietro Lorenzetti** have now been decontextualised and are kept elsewhere. Visiting the church, however, leads to the discovery of what an incredible museum of sculptures "in loco" is really like, with characteristics spanning over centuries in perfect harmony with the exterior decoration. Just inside the entrance visitors are welcomed at the top of the naves by a pair of holy water stoups by **Antonio Federighi** (1462–1463), which are typical examples of the classical style of the Renaissance. In the left nave the PICCOLOMINI ALTAR by the Lombard sculptor **Andrea Bregno** (1503) really stands out. It has some statues by **Michelangelo** in the niches and there is a *Madonna* painted by **Paolo di Giovanni Fei** above the table. **Lorenzo di Mariano** known as **Marrina** sculpted the monumental entrance to the PICCOLOMINI LIBRARY which stands out to the left. The Library was built by order of Francesco Piccolomini Todeschini in honour of his uncle Pius II and as a storage space for his rich collection of books. It is dominated by Pintoricchio's extremely vivid frescoes (1502-1507) which narrate episodes from the Pontiff's life but it also contains the famous sculptural grouping the *Three Graces*, a Roman copy of a Hellenistic original, and rare Renaissance illuminated antiphonies by **Girolamo da Cremona** and **Liberale da Verona**.

Going back into the nave you come to the CHAPEL OF ST. JOHN THE BAPTIST, which is also from the Renaissance and has a marble gateway by **Marrina**. The interior is decorated with sixteenth-century stuccoes and frescoes, some of which are by **Pintoricchio**, and a bronze statue of the Saint made in 1457 by **Donatello** stands in the central niche. A venerated relic of the arm of

St. John is kept behind the chapel. It was given to Siena Cathedral by Pope Pius II on the 6th May 1464 and was only ceremoniously displayed on the High Altar on the 24th June, the Baptist's Saint's Day. The relic was placed in a reliquary which can now be seen in the Museo dell'Opera del Duomo. It was commissioned from the goldsmith **Francesco d'Antonio** in 1465 and completed the year after. It is a splendid box in gilded silver decorated with scenes from the life of the Saint with pearls and precious stones which provide evidence of the splendour of goldsmithery at the time.

You can then move into the left transept, where the PULPIT can be seen above the hexagonal space marked out by the dome. This masterpiece of Gothic sculpture was made between 1266 and 1268 by **Nicola Pisano** with the help of his son **Giovanni** and his pupils **Arnolfo di Cambio**, **Donato** and **Lapo di Ricevuto**.

Francesco d'Antonio, *Reliquary of the arm St. John*, 1466, Siena, Museo dell'Opera
The Pulpit

The octagonal structure is supported by columns with the central one surrounded by a group of allegorical figures of the liberal arts. Christological stories run along the parapet – *Nativity*, *Adoration of the Magi*, *Presentation at the Temple*, *Crucifixion* and *Slaughter of the Innocents* – culminating in the *Universal Judgement* with Christ seated on a ridge between the two scenes of the blessed and the damned. Another noteworthy example of Gothic sculpture in this transept is the FUNERARY MONUMENT OF CARDINAL PETRONI by **Tino di Camaino** (1317–1318) which was reassembled here in 1951, while the *Tombstone of*

Lorenzo di Pietro known as Vecchietta,
Ciborium

Tino di Camaino, *Funeray Monument of
Cardinal Petroni*

Bishop Giovanni Pecci lies in the paving opposite. **Donatello** sculpted this
tombstone between 1426 and 1427 and he was able to create the illusion
of space and volume in the depth of the bronze with outstanding ability.
Unsurprisingly, the PRESBYTERY is dominated by the High Altar sculpted by
Baldassare Peruzzi in 1532, although it has retained a large bronze ciborium by **Lorenzo Vecchietta** (1467–1472) which was transferred here in 1506
from the Chiesa dell'Annunziata (Church of Our Lady of the Assumption)
inside the Hospital of Santa Maria della Scala. It sits in the centre of the
altar and is flanked by two pairs of angel candle holders. The lower pair are
the extremely refined work of **Francesco di Giorgio Martini**, while **Beccafumi** sculpted the eight angels on the pillar shelves.
Beccafumi also did the frescoes in the apse which were partly repainted after the earthquake in 1798, while a great, polychrome stained glass window
opens out above. This is a copy of **Duccio di Buoninsegna**'s original which is
now in the Museo dell'Opera.
A magnificent element of the apsidal area is the WOODEN CHOIR. The stalls
in the centre were made between 1567 and 1570 from drawings by **Riccio**,
while the fourteenth-century stalls at the sides by **Francesco** and **Jacopo del
Tonghio** have inlaid backs done by the Olivetan friar **Giovanni da Verona**
(1503) and were brought here at the beginning of the nineteenth century after
the dissolution of the Order's convent.

Going back via the right transept we come to the CHAPEL OF THE VOW (Cappella del Voto). This was a sparkling baroque addition planned in 1660 after a commission by Alessandro VII Chigi, although it was officially founded by his nephews Flavio and Agostino to house the ancient and venerated thirteenth-century image of the Madonna of the Graces which originated from **Guido da Siena**'s circle. From 1631 onwards the Chapel was named *of the Vow* after the solemn pledge made by the local government authorities to attend a sung Mass every Saturday to give thanks to the Madonna, who protected the city during the plague of 1630–1631. The area mirrors that of the Chapel of the Baptist and was constructed by the Sienese architect **Benedetto Giovannelli Orlandi**, although Gian Lorenzo Bernini was called on to oversee the sculptural ornamentation. He made the *St. James* and the *Magdalene* while *St. Bernardine* and *St. Catherine* were done by **Antonio Raggi** and **Ercole Ferrata** respectively. *The Visitation* by **Carlo Maratta** is on the left-hand wall and a mosaic with the *Flight from Egypt* by the same artist is on the right. This mosaic is an eighteenth-century copy of a painting by the artist who also made two large curved paintings on wood for the Sienese Chigi Chapel between 1661 and 1664.

Upon leaving the Chapel and moving towards the right nave there is a door which leads to the bell tower topped by the *Tomb of Bishop Tommaso Piccolomini del Testa*, sculpted by **Neroccio di Bartolomeo de' Landi** in 1484-85. The church's only side door opens out in the near corner. It is known as the door 'of Pardon' and a copy of the tondo with the *Madonna and Child (Madonna of Pardon)* by **Donatello**, intended for the destroyed Chapel of the Madonna of the Graces, is positioned above it on the outside. The original is conserved in the Museo dell'Opera.

The wooden choir
Donatello, *Madonna of Pardon*. Museo dell'Opera

36

There is a series of paintings by **Pier Dandini**, **Raffaello Vanni**, **Annibale Mazzuoli** and **Domenico Maria Canuti** on the seventeenth-century altars of the nave. The central gateway stands out on the counter-façade and the bases of its columns hold reliefs with *Stories of the Virgin* sculpted by **Urbano da Cortona** (1483). These were originally in the Chapel of the Madonna of the Graces, which was destroyed in 1658 along with the old archiepiscopal building right next to the Cathedral and then substituted two years later by the current Chapel of the Vow.

◇ 7 MUSEO DELL'OPERA

In order to really get to know the works of art created for the Cathedral, a visit to the Museo dell'Opera is practically essential. The museum houses the original sculptures that were once on the exterior of the building, the paintings that decorated the altars and the precious furnishings used to celebrate sacred rites. The richness of the works on display only adds to the fact that the museum's premises are in the first three bays of the abandoned New Cathedral's right nave. The museum visit also includes the atmospheric "facciatone" (great façade), a unique experience which offers one of the most enchanting panoramic views of the city. The museum came into being in 1869 and over time it has been enlarged to include the seventeenth-century Church of S. Niccolò, which is a rare example of baroque art in Siena. The visit starts in the SALA DELLA MADONNA DEGLI OCCHI GROSSI (ROOM OF THE MADONNA WITH THE BIG EYES) which takes its name from a thirteenth-century painting on wood used as an object of worship by the Sienese people when they came before it to trust in the protection of the Virgin Mary prior to the Battle of Montaperti. In the same room there is a polyptych by **Ambrogio Lorenzetti** and some interesting evidence of how painting was integrated into furniture. The panels for the wardrobes of the reliquaries and the books were made by **Benedetto di Bindo** at the beginning of the fifteenth century and the heads of the biers were painted by **Sodoma** a

The "Facciatone"

Maestro di Tressa, *Madonna of the Big Eyes*

little more than a century later.

The next room is the SALA ALFIERI, thus called because it was once a little theatre where some tragedies by the eighteenth-century poet were portrayed and he often visited the city. Aside from a series of fifteenth to seventeenth-century paintings there are two noteworthy polychrome terracotta sculptures attributed to **Domenico Beccafumi**.

In the following SALA DEGLI ARAZZI (ROOM OF THE TAPESTRIES) there are rich examples of tapestries with needlework which closely resembles the other figurative arts from the same era. Among other pieces, the priest's robes with the Chigi coat of arms are particularly interesting and their ornamentation can be linked to draw-

Roman Manufacture, *Chasuble*
Tuscan Manufacture, *Frontal*
The "Facciatone"

ings from **Bernini**'s workshop.

From this room visitors can go up to the terraces of the "FACCIATONE", that is to say the structure which should have become the façade of the magnificent new Cathedral planned in 1339. The view from both sides makes this a point of the visit not to be missed. (*PANORAMIC VIEW)

Moving on with the museum visit you come to the SALA DEL TESORO (ROOM OF THE TREASURE). Here you can admire a series of pieces which outline the ages of great Sienese goldsmithery from the end of the thirteenth century to the height of the fifteenth century with works by **Pace di Valentino**, **Ugolino di Vieri**, **Goro di ser**

The Golden Rose, from a design by Gian Lorenzo Bernini

Goro di Ser Neroccio, *Cope Clasp*

Duccio di Buoninsegna, *Maestà*, panels from the back: *The Wedding at Cana, Entrance into Jerusalem*

Neroccio and **Francesco d'Antonio**. The spectacular series of objects from Rome at the time of the Chigi papacy is no less important. It includes the *Golden Rose* from a design by **Bernini**, which has unfortunately lost its original impressive base as it was melted to cover restoration costs for the Cathedral's apse after the earthquake in 1798 and substituted with the current simpler, gilded copper version. From here visitors can reach one of the key rooms of the museum where the *Maestà* by **Duccio di Buoninsegna** is exhibited. It is a monumental two-sided painting on wood which was placed on the Cathedral's High Altar in 1311, although it was removed a relatively short time later at the beginning of the sixteenth century and then dismantled in 1771. As a consequence all the wooden pieces which made up the frame were lost and when the work was transferred to the new museum in 1878 some painted parts had also disappeared. Only eight of them have since reappeared in foreign collections.

The imposing ensemble on the front is an *Enthroned Madonna and Child* surrounded by a host of angels and saints with the four patron saints of Siena kneeling in the foreground – Ansanus, Savinus, Crescentius and Victor. On the step up to the throne there is an inscription with an entreaty to the Virgin Mary for peace in Siena and also "life" to Duccio to thank him for having painted her so well: "*Mater Sancta Dei Sis Causa Senis Requiei – Sis Ducio Vita Te Quia Pinxit Ita*". The large central composition was completely surrounded by scenes with *Stories of the Virgin* alternated with images of prophets and apostles which are now exhibited separately and they are characterised by exceptional chromatic and narrative liveliness.

The large central composition was completely surrounded by scenes with *Stories of the Virgin* alternated with images of prophets and apostles which are now exhibited separately. The panels which were on the back of the polyptych with episodes from the *Passion of Christ* are also exhibited separately and are characterised by exceptional chromatic and narrative liveliness.

There is another masterpiece in this room which, due to changing tastes, was removed from the altar it was intended for: **Pietro Lorenzetti** painted the *Nativity of the Virgin* in 1342 for the Altar of St. Savinus in the corner chapel of the Cathedral's left transept. The artist makes this sacred event relevant by setting it in an interior from the time along with the masterly use of customs and costumes and also the expressive mood of the various figures.

The following room, SALA JACOPO DELLA QUERCIA, still has sixteenth-century wooden panelling by **Bartolomeo Neroni** known as **Riccio**. It holds a group of statues sculpted in wood by **Jacopo della Quercia** between 1419

Duccio di Buoninsegna, *Maestà*, front and back

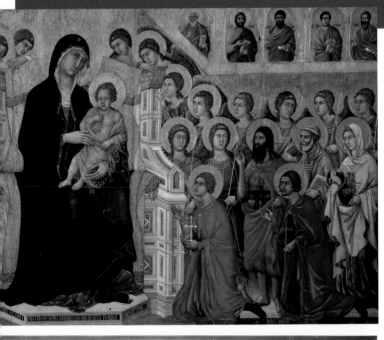

and 1425 for the Church of S. Martino. Masterpieces of Sienese wooden sculpture, particularly the *Sorrowful* by **Domenico di Niccolò dei Cori**, can also be found in the adjacent SALA DEL CROCIFISSO (ROOM OF THE CROSS).

The visit continues into the SALA DEI CARTONI (ROOM OF THE CARTOONS), thus called because there are nineteenth-century drawings on display that reproduce the marble decoration of the Cathedral's paving and also be-

Pietro Lorenzetti, *Nativity of the Virgin*, 1442

Jacopo della Quercia, *Madonna and Child with Saints*

cause it holds a series of illuminated choir books. Above all it gives a particularly significant impression of what the New Cathedral would have been like inside.

The Galleria delle Statue (Gallery of Statues), the Sala del Portale Centrale (Room of the Central Gateway) and the Sala degli Apostoli (Room of the Apostles) leave an even stronger impression on visitors as they contain a charming series of sculptures by **Giovanni Pisano** and his school which were once on the exterior of the Cathedral. More recently the large, circular, polychrome stained glass window from the apse made at around the same time by **Duccio di Buoninsegna** has been added to the collection. The visit comes to an end in the Church of S. Niccolò, which is a perfect example of the combination of architecture, painting and plastic ornamentation in seventeenth-century art.

Santa Maria della Scala is one of the most ancient sites of pilgrim hospitality in Siena as it had already become a stopping point along the Via Francigena in the ninth century and until very recently it still had some hospital treatment facilities.. It is an imposing monumental complex which gives visitors a taste of a real journey through time and history and the experience is rendered even more fascinating by the two-storey descent under the ground level of Piazza del Duomo next to the VIA DEL FOSSO DI SANT'ANSANO (ST. ANSANUS' DITCH). The Ditch can be reached through an internal, covered passage providing unique evidence of medieval urban practicality. The Santa Maria della Scala complex is also steadily finding space for all the civic museums of the city like, for example, the BAMBIMUS – MUSEUM OF ART FOR CHILDREN in the Sale della Spezieria and the Sala San Leopoldo, the CENTRO D'ARTE CONTEMPORANEA in the Palazzo delle Papesse and the MUSEO ARCHEOLOGICO STATALE. A plan to include the NATIONAL ART GALLERY (PINACOTECA NAZIONALE) is also in progress, thus putting into effect the idea of a single, large group of museums all in the same place.

The entrance is opposite the Cathedral and the CAPPELLA DEL MANTO (CHAPEL OF THE MANTLE) sits next to the foyer. The Cappella del Manto takes its name

from the fresco of the *Madonna of Mercy* made for it in 1444 by **Domenico di Bartolo** (detached in 1610 and placed in the Old Sacristy). The Chapel, however, was originally built to hold the prestigious relics from Constantinople bought by the Hospital in 1459 whose precious reliquaries are among the most important works of art in the museum. The PELLE-GRINAIO (PILGRIM'S LODGE) sits on the other side of the Museum's foyer, the place where pilgrims originally came to stay. It was built in the second half of the fourteenth century and frescoed during the following century with a pictorial cycle designed by the then rector of the Francesco Buzzichelli Hospital who wanted to celebrate the history and the purpose of the institution. Starting with the first scene on the left there is a work by **Lorenzo Vecchietta** (1441 ca) with Blessed Sorore's mother. Blessed Sorore was the renowned founder of the hospital whose mother, during her pregnancy, dreamed of her son's commitment to this undertaking, destined in part to aban-

Lorenzo Vecchietta, *The dream of Blessed Sorore's mother*, 1441

47

doned children. On the opposite wall there is a fresco of *The Offering of the Bishop* by **Domenico di Bartolo** who – between 1440 and 1444 – painted the scenes with *The Celestial Pontiff concedes the privilege of autonomy on the Hospital, the "government" and the healing of the sick, The distribution of "offerings", Reception, education and marriage of a daughter of the Hospital* and *The lunch of the poor.* **Priamo della Quercia**, the brother of the more well-known sculptor, made the *Investiture of the Rector of the Hospital* (1442) while the Florentine, late-mannerist painters **Pietro d'Achille Crogi** and **Giovanni di Raffale Navesi** made the two scenes with *The payment of the "wet nurses" with wheat and with money* between 1575 and 1577 after the enlargement of the *Pellegrinaio* towards the *valle* area.

Another particularly interesting area is the Sagrestia Vecchia (Old Sacristy) known as the Cappella del Sacro Chiodo (Chapel of the Sacred Nail) as it was built to house the venerated relics owned by the hospital. Among the relics the one which certainly would have stood out from the rest due to its exceptional nature was a nail from the crucifixion of Christ. It was so exceptional in fact, that it determined the subject of the frescoes, which were centred on the *Articles of the Creed* and made between 1446 and 1449 by **Vecchietta**. Vecchietta had previously been commissioned to make the *Arliquiera*, the wardrobe for the relics which is now on display in the National Art Gallery. The outstanding nature of this container is in consequence of its exceptional contents, now referred to as the Treasure of Santa Maria della Scala. This collection of relics is

Domenico di Bartolo, *Reception, education and marriage of a daughter of the Hospital,* 1441-1442

Reliquary of the Sacred Nail, second half of the 14th century

Lorenzo di Pietro known as Vecchietta, *Christ Resurrected*

believed to have come directly from the imperial chapel of Constantinople and the objects still constitute the image which is most associated with the Hospital today. They were valued at the incredible sum of 3000 fiorini when Santa Maria della Scala bought them in 1359 through a merchant from Signa living in Venice. Besides the abovementioned Sacred Nail, which previously belonged to the emperor Constantine, there is also a fragment of wood from the True Cross found by St. Helen, which the Virgin Mary dropped from her waist into the hands of St. Thomas as proof of her assumption. These relics of faith became the cultural heart of the institution and were only exhibited with full ceremony on the day of the Annunciation and paraded through the town in times of danger when people felt the need to appeal to their thaumaturgic properties to guarantee prestige and generous donations for the Hospital. To this existing value we can add the artistic worth of their precious containers. Among the oldest ones the gilded silver and enamel lid of the evangeliary stands out. It topped the list of the objects from Constantinople while among the ones added to the collection later on, the *Arm-reliquary of St. Biagio* by **Goro di Ser Neroccio** in 1437 and the series of reliquary busts also from the fourteenth century must not be forgotten.

The Chapel of the Sacred Nail was built right next to the ancient Church of the Santissima Annunziata which was altered shortly after to take on a Renaissance form. The high altar holds the magnificent and prominent *Christ Resurrected* signed by **Lorenzo Vecchietta** in 1476. The fresco in the apse depicting *Probatica Piscina* was painted in 1730 by **Sebastiano Conca**. The church also contains a precious organ from the early fifteenth century by **Giovanni di maestro Antonio "Piffaro"**.

The Pellegrinaio delle Donne (Women's Pilgrim Hospice) was built in the

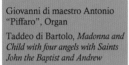

Giovanni di maestro Antonio "Piffaro", Organ

Taddeo di Bartolo, *Madonna and Child with four angels with Saints John the Baptist and Andrew*

middle of the fourteenth century and contains frescoes by **Martino di Bartolomeo** and others ascribed to **Bartolo di Fredi** and **Andrea di Bartolo**. Moving down to the first lower ground floor visitors find themselves in the CORTICELLA (LITTLE COURTYARD), an original fourteenth-century area recuperated thanks to restorations which is an interconnecting point of the visit. From here visitors can accede to the area which was once a barn where a restoration project is currently in progress focusing on what is left of the Fonte Gaia. The worksite is open to the public and provides a point of comparison with plaster casts taken by Sarrocchi to prepare the copy which was placed in Piazza del Campo in 1868. After the restoration is completed it will also be the final display location of **Jacopo della Quercia**'s sculptural grouping.

The ORATORIO DELLA COMPAGNIA DI SANTA CATERINA DELLA NOTTE (ORATORY OF THE COMPANY OF ST. CATHERINE OF THE NIGHT) sits next to this area. It is an evocative chapel where the Saint came to pray and it was decorated during the eighteenth century with stuccoes and paintings depicting stories from her life. The altar, on the other hand, holds a sculpted fourteenth-century *Madonna* while among the various works of art in the sacristy the triptych with the *Madonna and Child with four angels and Saints John the Baptist and Andrew* signed by **Taddeo di Bartolo** in 1400 is noteworthy. Moving back into the *Corticella* visitors can pass through another room to enter the ORATORY OF THE COMPANY OF ST. MARY UNDER THE VAULTS OF THE HOSPITAL which then became the SOCIETY OF EXECUTORS OF PIOUS DISPOSITIONS. This Society still has a plentiful and noteworthy artistic collection although most of it is in their premises in Via Roma. Just behind a wall cavity in an entrance way to the Oratory, which was removed during a restoration project, an important cycle of frescoes depicting a *Thebaid* attributed to **Ambrogio Lorenzetti**'s circle was found. The MAGAZZINI DELLA

Ambrogio Lorenzetti, *Thebaid* (detail)

Attic amphora with black figures and maenads, satyrs and a chariot

CORTICELLA (STOREROOMS OF THE LITTLE COURTYARD) are also interesting from a spatial point of view and they are now used as an exhibition area. From the *Corticella* visitors can go down to the so-called LABYRINTHS on the second lower ground floor where the MUSEO ARCHEOLOGICO NAZIONALE ETRUSCO is now situated. The museum was founded in 1933 by the famous archaeologist Ranuccio Bianchi Bandinelli who was born in Siena. The organisation of the museum highlights the initial nucleus of the collection which came from other local collections around the end of the nineteenth century and the beginning of the twentieth century. The findings range from the Bronze Age to the Etruscan and Roman eras and constitute the most prestigious pieces of work in the whole museum like, for example, the golden fibula from the seventh century BC, the series of red Etruscan ceramics, various antefixes from the sixth to the forth centuries BC and the urns from the Hellenistic-Roman era from the Cumere family hypogeum. This first part of the visit is flanked by a more educational topographic section which illustrates the Sienese territory from the eleventh century BC onwards, subdividing it into cultural areas.

THE PALIO

Siena's identity is linked to the Palio just as much as to its historic urban situation and its artistic vestiges from the past.

The origins of the Palio are traditionally linked to the year 1260 as a celebration of the victory over the Florentines in the battle of Montaperti but in reality the modern Palio is the result of unification of various races and their rules which were organised in the past. In particularly, the two fixed dates of the current race can be traced back to the end of the sixteenth century as regards the Palio on the 2nd July, and 1701 as regards the one on the 16th August.

The seventeen 'contrade' or districts of Siena which compete in the Palio are: Aquila (Eagle), Bruco (Caterpillar), Chiocciola (Snail), Civetta (Owl), Drago (Dragon), Giraffa (Giraffe), Istrice (Porcupine), Leocorno (Unicorn), Lupa (She-Wolf), Nicchio (Seashell), Oca (Goose), Onda (Wave), (Pantera) Panther, Selva (Forest), Tartuca (Tortoise), Torre (Tower) and Valdimontone (Ram). Only ten districts, however, participate in each race with a system of rotation based on a rule emitted in 1720. Both Palio races are dedicated to the Vir-

Vincenzo Rustici (copy from the 18th century), *Parade of the districts in Piazza del Campo*. Palazzo Pubblico

gin Mary, the protectress of the city, and they are celebrated in connection with her two Saint's days – the local one of the miraculous, venerated image in the Basilica of Provenzano and the Assumption. It is a horse race which takes place around the Piazza del Campo and the hero of the event is really the horse. The horse can win the race even if it arrives at the finish line after the jockey has fallen off and it is the horse which gets taken triumphantly into the church of the winning district.

The winning district receives a prize which was originally a precious fabric flag called the palio. For a long time now this has been a painted banner called the *drappellone* (large flag). In 1910 the people decided to hold a competition to decide who would make the banner among the students of the local Institute of Art and the winner would be rewarded with one hundred lira.

The first person to be chosen was eighteen-year-old **Aldo Piantini** who made both banners for that year and also those of the Palio of the Assumption in 1911 and 1913 and finally the one for the race held in Provenanzo in 1919 to celebrate Italy's victory in the Second World War, during which the Palio had obviously been suspended. From 1970 onwards it became standard practice to alternate the creator of the two banners for the two annual Palio races with a Sienese artist and a renowned international artist. In recent years some of the artists have been **Emilio Tadini, Jean Michel Folon** and **Jim Dine**.

Aldo Piantini, *"Drappellone" from the Palio of July 1910*. Museo della Contrada di Valdimontone

The presentation of the banner takes place in the Courtyard of the Podestà six days before the race and being there is a unique experience because the tension of anticipation can be felt among the thronging crowd of people from the various districts. This tension dissolves into applause or hissing the moment the image is revealed. In actual fact it is not easy to unite the motives of art with the traditions of the Palio, and the prevalence of a symbolic colour of one of the districts is enough to provoke a dispute.

Emilio Tadini, *"Drappellone" from the Palio of July 1997*. Museo della Contrada della Giraffa

The oldest, original Palio in existence is the one that was won on the 2nd July 1719 by the Nobile Contrada dell'Aquila (District of the Eagle). It is on display in the museum of the district on the corner of Via del Casato di Sotto in rooms adjoining the Church of St. John the Baptist. This Church was built in 1629 for the Brotherhood of the Tredicini but became the Oratory of the Eagle in 1788. Other banners, even some from the previous century, are recorded with copies and exhibited with pride by the various winning districts of the time. Another prize awarded for the Palio is a silver platter called *masgalano* – in Spanish *mas galante* – which singles out the most elegant district in the procession through the town. The two oldest ones were awarded in 1658 and 1701 respectively and are part of the Contrada della Tartuca's (District of the Tortoise's) collection of memorabilia on display in the museum next to their oratory in Via Tommaso Pendola. The oratory was built by the district in 1682 and is dedicated to St. Anthony of Padua. Unlike other places where similar competitions are held, daily life in Siena is influenced by the Palio for the whole year. The Anno Contradaiolo (District Year) starts on the 1st December which is the Saint's Day of St. Ansanus, the evangeliser of the city. On this day the 17 Contrade form a procession from the Piazza del Campo to the Cathedral where the Archbishop celebrates a solemn Mass at the altar of the Saint. Among the various other ceremonies which take place throughout the city, the Corteo dei Ceri e dei Censi (Procession of Candles) on the 14th August must not be forgotten. The procession starts at the church of St. George in Via di Pantaneto with the candles which each district and parish offers to the Virgin Mary. This religious parade joins the city authorities in front of the Chiasso Largo before proceeding together to the Cathedral where, in front of the Chapel of the Vow, the Mayor lights a candle on behalf of the Municipality for the protectress of the city. During the ceremony of the candle, the banner for the Palio on the 16th August is blessed.

ALONG THE WAY

Depending on the way people come into Siena and their form of transport, the itineraries to reach the heart of the city will take them past buildings, churches, works of arts and various panoramic views. The following pages illustrate the itineraries in detail so that visitors can give preference to their interests and organise their time accordingly.

◇
1 CHURCH OF S. DOMENICO

For those who arrive in Siena by bus from Florence or Rome and also for those who park their cars in the area around the stadium or the Medici Fortress, the approach to the old town centre starts with the Church of St. Domenic, an imposing Gothic brickwork structure. Building work began in 1226 but the church was not completed until over two centuries later and then repeatedly subjected to renovations and restorations. The site is particularly linked to the worship of St. Catherine, the Sienese Saint who was born and lived in the surrounding area and belonged, from 1352 onwards, to the Third Dominican Order known as the Sisters of the Mantellate. At the time the Order had the use of the CAPPELLA DELLE VOLTE (CHAPEL OF THE VAULTS) on the counter-facade of the church. Here, among the various paintings with stories of the Saint, there is portrait which is considered to be her faithful likeness by her contemporary and follower **Andrea Vanni**.

Venerated relics of the Saint are on display in a reliquary next to the right-hand wall of the nave, before the entrance to the cloister and the subsequent CAPPELLA DI S. CATERINA (CHAPEL OF ST. CATHERINE). Building work on the Chapel began in 1466 in a Renaissance style, including the decorative paving in inlaid marble dubiously ascribed to **Francesco di Giorgio**. It was finished off during the sixteenth century with frescoes by **Sodoma** (1526) and **Francesco Vanni** (1593–1596).

The head of the Saint is conserved in a marble tabernacle on the altar by Giovanni di Stefano (1466). On her Saint's Day, the 29th April, it is brought with full ceremony to the Piazza del Campo where Italy and Europe are blessed with the relic since St. Catherine is their joint patron saint.

The following wall is dominated by a detached fresco by **Pietro Lorenzetti** depicting a *Madonna and Child, St John the Baptist and a knight*. There is also a painting with the *Adoration of the Shepherds* by **Francesco di Giorgio Martini** and **Bernardino Fungai**. An *Our Lady of the Assumption* by **Sodoma** and remains of fifteenth-century frescoes can be found in the SACRISTY. In the right nave there are fragmentary frescoes from **Lippo Vanni**'s circle, a *Madonna and Saints* by **Matteo di Giovanni** (1476) and a unique series of "German tombs", sixteenth and seventeenth-century funerary monuments of Germans who died in the city, especially students from the prestigious local university. A ciborium stands on the High Altar flanked by angels by **Benedetto da Maiano** (1475–1480), a refined example of Renaissance marble holy vessels, while modern stained glass windows by **Bruno Cassinari** light up the apse. Along with other contemporary artists Bruno Cassinari also provided the drawings for the new windows decorated with figures. In the chapels of the left nave important works include the wooden statue of *St. Anthony Abbot* by **Francesco di Valdambrino**, a late fifteenth-century crucifix, and more especially, the Maestà by **Guido da Siena** in the centre chapel which can be traced back to 1270–1275. The year 1221 in the signature inscription has allowed the work to be considered as the "founder" of Sienese painting and a precursor to the Florentine genre although in reality it is most probably a vestige of a previous venerated image. In the Gothic crypt there is a fifteenth-century painted cross by **Sano di Pietro** and a *Crucifixion* signed in 1600 by **Ventura Salimbeni**. On the 17th January, the Saint's Day of St. Anthony Abbot, the rite of the blessing of the animals takes place here as the reclusive Saint is their traditional protector.

From S. Domenico you can follow Via della Sapienza but then turn immediately to the right into Costa S. Antonio to reach the ST. CATHERINE'S SANCTUARY.

◇
2 ST. CATHERINE'S SANCTUARY

OTHER VIEWS

"In Siena you can see the house where Catherine of Siena used to live, now transformed into a church. The room where Jesus Christ appeared before her is a chapel and behind it, they say, is the room where she slept with the bricks she used as a pillow covered in silver."
MARQUIS DE SADE, *Voyage to Italy*, Paris, 1776

The place where Caterina Benincasa used to live was transformed into a sanctuary and it is a frequent destination for pilgrimages. It is also a historical stopping point for every traveller passing through Siena even if they do not have religious faith. The fact that this well-known libertine chose to refer to the mystical union of Catherine with Christ does not appear to be without ambiguous implied meanings, associating her ascetic visions with the description of her bed. The figure of St. Catherine, however, does exert a strong sense of fascination. She was a mystical Saint but had great intellectual capacity – so much so that she was proclaimed a Doctor of the Church – and she was able to use her skill with words to induce Pope Gregory XI to bring the papal seat from Avignon back to Rome.

The complex can be accessed through a neo-Renaissance structure made in 1941, two years after Catherine was named as a patron of Italy and it includes the Saint's place of birth, bought by the municipality in 1466. The internal courtyard has two open galleries. The oldest one was designed by **Giovan Battista Pelori** (1530–1550) following the style of **Baldassarre Peruzzi**.

The entrance to the CHURCH OF CROCIFISSO (CHURCH OF THE CROSS) is on the right and its altar holds a painted cross from the late twelfth century. Catherine actually received the stigmata before this altar in 1375 in the Pisan Church of St. Christina, hence its transferral to Siena in 1565 by order of Cosimo de' Medici. The ORATORIO DELLA CUCINA (ORATORY OF THE KITCH-

Painted Cross, Pisan School, late 12th century

EN) was originally the kitchen of Catherine's family home and then the first seat of the non-clerical society dedicated to her. It still has a late Renaissance majolica-tiled floor and a coffered wooden ceiling, while the walls are covered in paintings mainly by sixteenth-century artists (**Alessandro Casolani, Cristofano Roncalli, Pietro Sorri, Bartolomeo Riccio, Francesco Vanni**) but also some from the following century (**Rutilio Manetti**) and the nineteenth century (**Pietro Aldi** and **Gaetano Marinelli**).

In the Saint's bedroom, where the stone she laid her head on to sleep still lies, there is a painting on wood by **Giovanni di Benvenuto** depicting *St. Catherine receiving the stigmata* and frescoes with seven *Stories* from her life painted by **Alessandro Franchi** and **Gaetano Marinelli** (1896).

Ventura Salimbeni,
St. Catherine depicted with other Sienese Saints in the act of protecting the town.
Cathedral, fresco

Further down visitors reach the cellar where, as tradition has it, there was always a miraculously full bottle of wine. The ORATORIO DELLA TINTORIA or S. CATERINA IN FONTEBRANDA (ORATORY OF THE DYEWORKS OR ST. CATHERINE IN FONTEBRANDA) is also the Oratory of the Contrada dell'Oca (District of the Goose). It was built in 1465–74 where the warehouse of the Benincasa family once stood, as the Saint's father Jacopo had a clothes dying business. The interior walls were completely frescoed at the beginning of the sixteenth century and during the following century with stories of the Saint. There is also a beautiful wooden statue of Catherine by **Neroccio di Bartolomeo** (1474).

Once outside in Vicolo del Tiratoio you can move up towards Piazza del Campo along Via della Galluzza crossing Via di Diacceto and then going into Via di Beccheria. All these street names are reminiscent of the activities which once took place in them – the manufacture of textiles, the ice factory and the selling of poultry and meat. The area is charmingly marked with evidence of these occupations through the medieval road lay-out with arches and running balconies between the houses and a maze of little alleyways like Vicolo della Macina and Vicolo delle Carrozze, which are well worth a deviation.

You then come into Via di Città practically in front of one of the short, steep slopes down into Piazza del Campo.

Retracing your steps…
After completing itinerary **0** (see pgs. 12–51) you can leave Piazza del Duomo along Via del Capitano to reach
3 PIAZZA DELLA POSTIERLA (see pgs. 87–88) before turning left into Via di Città to reach
4 PALAZZO DELLE PAPESSE (see p. 77) and
5 PALAZZO CHIGI SARACINI (see pgs. 75–77) and follow it until
6 LOGGIA DELLA MERCANZIA (see p. 71) and the Croce del Travaglio (see p. 71), where you can turn left into Banchi di Sopra until
7 PIAZZA SALIMBENI (see p. 68) to then go back up the short Via Pianigiani which leads to Piazza Matteotti.

S. CATERINA DEL PARADISO (ST. CATHERINE OF PARADISE) stands at the top of a flight of steps in the left-hand corner. It was built between 1620 and 1626 and from 1787 onwards it has been the Oratory of the Contrada del Drago (District of the Dragon). There are various paintings inside from the same era as its construction as well as two polychrome terracottas from the early sixteenth century by **Lorenzo Mariano** known as **Marrina**.

From the square that leads to the stadium you can simply go up an incline to the left to reach The "Lizza" Gardens (GIARDINI DELLA LIZZA). From the car parks around the Fortress visitors must go straight on and then bear left to reach these gardens.

8 THE "LIZZA" GARDENS

The name "La Lizza" derives from the original purpose of this area for horse races but by the end of the eighteenth century it had been transformed into a garden. This transformation was carried out by the engineer **Antonio Matteucci** in collaboration with the German **Leopoldo Prucher**, the head gardener of the Boboli gardens in Florence, and together they managed to create an area at one with the sixteenth-century Medici Fortress.

9 THE MEDICI FORTRESS

The fortress was built by order of Cosimo I de' Medici after Siena's final capitulation in 1560. Its purpose was to preside over potential revolts in the city so for Sienese people it was an intolerable symbol of Florentine rule.
The structure stands in place of the Spanish fort destroyed by the Sienese in 1552 when they momentarily regained independence. It was modified from its

⑨

original "L" shape to the square shape we can still see today, designed by the military architect **Baldassarre Lanci**. In 1777 Pietro Leopoldo completely de-militarised it, winning great popularity with the Sienese people. He entrusted the restructuring of the fortress into a public walking place to the architect of the Royal Factories of the Grand Duchy **Zanobi del Rosso** and the area was inaugurated in 1779.

On the 17th August 1874 a special Palio called "alla Romana" was held in the internal square of the fortress. An "alla Romana" race meant a Palio ran by the winners of a series of preliminary heats.

In addition to the green areas around the outside, the internal part of the fortress is now also a place for relaxation, particularly thanks to the presence of the Enoteca Italiana and the Siena Jazz association which organise various events at different times of the year. (*PANORAMIC VIEW)

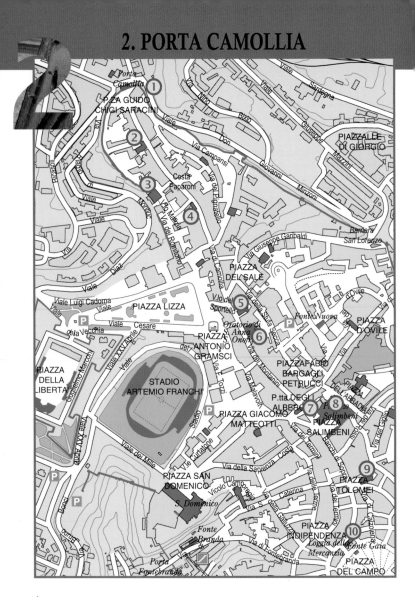

◇ 1 PORTA CAMOLLIA

If you arrive by train and take the bus into the centre you can get off near Porta Camollia – the historic entrance to the city from the direction of Florence along Via Cassia. The gate welcomes visitors with the inscription *Cor magis tibi Sena pandit* : "With the heart [of this gate] Siena opens out before you". Passing under the arch, which can be traced back to the reconstruction in 1604, you can follow Via di Camollia to reach the CHURCH OF S. PIETRO ALLA MAGIONE (St. Peter at Home).

◇ 2 CHURCH OF S. PIETRO ALLA MAGIONE

This church is documented from the tenth century and was originally linked to the hospital of the Templars but it has been repeatedly altered over time. It holds works of art from various eras including frescoes by **Lippo Vanni**. Further ahead,

on the same side of the street, the FONTEGIUSTA arch leads down towards the CHURCH OF S. MARIA IN PORTICO A FONTEGIUSTA.

◇ 3 CHURCH OF S. MARIA IN PORTICO A FONTEGIUSTA

The façade of this church really stands out against the skyline. Building work started in 1479 in an act of thanksgiving to the Madonna for the victory over Florence at Poggio Imperiale in the same year. It has retained its Renaissance character both on the outside, particularly shown by the marble gateway from 1489, and in the almost square interior, marked out by columns into three naves covered by cross vaults.

On the altar there is a miraculous image of the *Madonna di Fontegiusta* which has been there since 1806. It is part of a fresco originally from the portico of the customs house which was incorporated into the church. Noteworthy paintings among the works of art include a fresco by **Daniele da Volterra** depicting *The Tiburtine Sibyl predicts the birth of Christ to Augustus*.

Going back onto Via Camollia you come to the CHURCH OF SS. VINCENZO E ANASTASIO (St. Vincent and Anastasius).

◇ 4 CHURCH OF SS. VINCENZO E ANASTASIO

The Umbrian artist Pintoricchio was buried here in 1513. Siena Cathedral proudly holds one of his most famous pictorial cycles in the Piccolomini Library.

THE PALIO

The Church of SS. Vincenzo e Anastasio has been the Oratory of the Contrada Sovrana dell'Istrice (District of the Porcupine) since 1788. Previously it had used Fonteguista Oratory. Besides the banners won in the Palio, the nearby museum holds an early thirteenth-century fresco depicting Christ Benedictory which was originally on the building's exterior and is thought to be one of the oldest in the city. The museum also has a *Madonna* painted by **Sano di Pietro** and precious sacred silverware and vestments.

◇
5 Church of S. Andrea

The itinerary continues along Via dei Montanini where this church of medieval origin can be seen. It has been completely altered over time excepting the exterior of the apse, although it contains many interesting paintings such as the triptych on the High Altar signed by **Giovanni di Paolo** and dated 1445.

◇
6. Oratory of S. Anna in S. Onofrio

This Oratory stands a short distance ahead and can be traced back to the fourteenth century. It was renovated, however, in the eighteenth century and many of the paintings and statues inside are from this era, except the *Bust in polychrome terracotta of St. Bernardine*, which can be dated to the latter fifteenth century and was originally on the exterior to mark the place of the Saint's first sermon in Siena.

Just before the end of Via dei Montanini the Piazzetta degli Alberghi opens out to the right. This was once a stopping point on the Via Francigena and it is immediately followed by S. Maria delle Nevi (St. Mary of the Snow).

◇
7 S. Maria delle Nevi

This elegant Renaissance building was built between 1470 and 1472 by order of **Giovanni de' Cinughi**, the Bishop of Pienza and Montalcino. It is characterised by a general sense uniformity with refined partitions and ornamentation and it benefits from an accreditation to **Francesco di Giorgio**. Inside on

the High Altar there is an image of the *Madonna of the Snow* painted by **Matteo di Giovanni** (1477) which is considered to be one of his masterpieces.

◇
8 PIAZZA SALIMBENI

This square opens out on the opposite side of the street a little further ahead. It was constructed at the end of the nineteenth century in a historicist reinterpretation aimed at allowing the Gothic building of the same name to be more prominent. The square came into being around the site of the mansion which has been linked to this powerful Ghibelline family since the twelfth century. It was enlarged and restructured in 1880 and is currently the premises of the Monte dei Paschi di Siena bank, one of the oldest banks in the world. The bank was founded as Monte Pio in 1472 and over time it has brought together an important collection of works of art (only open to visitors upon request) including the *Madonna of Mercy* commissioned to **Benvenuto di Giovanni** in 1481 to celebrate the anniversary of its foundation.

Benvenuto di Giovanni, *Madonna of Mercy*

68

The name of the street you are now walking along is Banchi di Siena, a name which reflects the previous presence of money changers and merchants in this area. A short distance ahead on the right-hand side you come to PIAZZA TOLOMEI which is overlooked by a building of the same name. Palazzo Tolomei was built in the thirteenth century by the powerful Guelph family, known by everyone at the time because of the figure of Pia immortalised by Dante in *Purgatory*. It is one of the oldest private buildings still standing in the city and it is currently the premises of the Florentine bank the Cassa di Risparmio di Firenze.

Palazzo Tolomei

◊
9 CHURCH OF S. CRISTOFORO

This church sits on the other side of the square. It has roman origins but it was renovated in 1720 and then again in 1800 when the current brickwork façade was constructed. Only the twelfth-century cloister remains from the original structure but even that was restored in 1921. Visitors gain access from Via del Moro where, as tradition has it, the Sienese poet **Cecco Angiolieri** who was a contemporary of Dante is buried. This poet was extremely well-known for his invective verses, especially the sonnet *"S'i fossi foco arderei lo mondo"* (*If I were fire I would burn the world*), which was put to music and sung in 1968 by the Italian singer Fabrizio de André. Inside the church there is a polychrome terracotta sculptural grouping in the style of **Jacopo della Quercia** and a *St. George and the Dragon* attributed to the **Master of the Osservanza**. The significance of this place is linked more to Siena's civil history than to art as the city government met here before the Palazzo Pubblico was built and it was here that the Gran Consiglio made the decision to go to battle against the Florentines at Montaperti in 1260, which turned out to be a historical victory over their long-term enemies.

Piazza Tolomei, column of the She-Wolf

The Colonna con la Lupa (Column of the She-Wolf) rises up in the square and is a civic symbol marking out the *terzieri*, that is to say the three areas into which the city was once divided.

The street ends at the Croce del Travaglio, a crucial crossroads between Banchi di Sopra, Banchi di Sotto and Via di Città as these are the three roads that come together to link the three hills the urban city centre is built on. The Loggia della Mercanzia (The Loggia of Merchandise) stands opposite.

Croce del Travaglio

◇◇ 10 Loggia della Mercanzia

This structure can be traced back to the fifteenth century and it is characterised by pillars with inhabited niches. Four of the niches hold alternate sculptures by **Vecchietta** and **Federighi** (two of which are in Santa Maria della Scala for conservation reasons and have been substituted by copies). The vaulting has elegant sixteenth-century ornamentation – along with extensive, further work carried out in the nineteenth century – which interconnects stuccoes and painting.

At the corner of the Loggia the Vicolo S. Pietro leads down into Piazza del Campo.

Retracing your steps…

After completing itinerary **0** (see pgs. 12–51) visitors can chose to retrace their steps by leaving Piazza del Duomo by Via dei Fusari and after Piazza del Battistero turning left into the enchanting Via di Diacceto. Turning left again into Via della Galluzza visitors can then follow itinerary **1** –from Via della Galluzza to S. Domenico (see pgs. 56–63) – to reach Piazza Gramsci where several buses pass on their way to the station.

Via di Diacceto

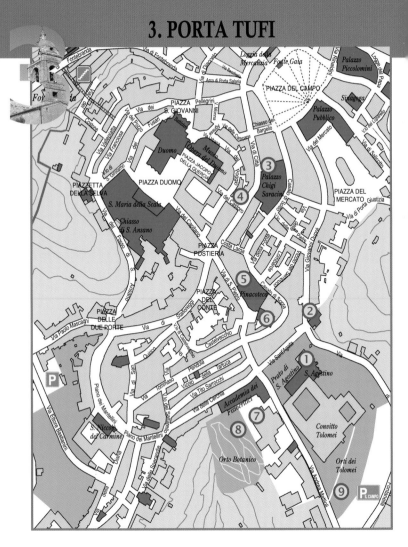

If you arrive by car and leave it in the "Il Campo" car park just inside Porta Tufi, the Prato di S. Agostino, which takes its name from the sacred building on the right, is just a short distance away.

◇
1 CHURCH OF S. AGOSTINO

This church is now used for cultural events. This medieval building was transformed in 1487 by the addition of the chapel in the right transept, then again in the middle of the eighteenth century with an internal renovation entrusted to **Luigi Vanvitelli** and finally in 1819 with the construction of the entrance gateway designed by **Agostino Fantastici**. At the same time the adjacent convent which had been dissolved in 1808, was converted into a secondary school.

The paintings here include particularly interesting monochrome frescoes by **Francesco di Giorgio Martini** and **Luca Signorelli** found during restoration work in the 1970s in the chapel of the transept, and a painting on wood with the *Crucifixion* by **Perugino** (1503–1506) on the second right-hand altar. Other noteworthy works include the wooden choir from 1630 and various sculptures such as the *Madonna del Magnificat* attributed to **Giovanni di Turino** on the altar of the presbytery's first right-hand chapel, and the *Funerary monument of Agostino Chigi* made in 1631 by **Tommaso Redi** in the left arm of the transept. The PICCOLOMINI CHAPEL can be accessed from the nave and was once the convent's chapterhouse. In 1946 a fresco depicting the *Madonna and Child* which can be ascribed to **Ambrogio Lorenzetti**'s circle was found here and it also contains an imposing painting on wood with the *Adoration of the Magi* painted by **Sodoma** around 1530.

BEYOND THE GATE

Hermitage of Lecceto

The Augustinian order is also historically linked to what used to be two important places of retreat near the city, Lecceto and S. Leonardo al Lago, both of which are set in magnificent countryside.

The HERMITAGE OF LECCETO is 8 kilometres west of Siena. Documentary evidence of this settlement dates from 1220 but as tradition has it was already in existence in the forth century as Augustine is said to have spent part of his life here after being baptised by St. Ambrose. Various Popes are also said to have lived there as well as William Flete, a former scholar of the University of Cambridge who became confessor and advisor to St. Catherine. The church was rebuilt in 1317 in the place of a pre-existing structure. It was subsequently enlarged and then transformed entirely to take on a baroque form. The gateway still holds traces of fifteenth-century monochrome frescoes but the frescoes in the cloister are even more interesting. They are situated, however, in a closed off area.

S. LEONARDO AL LAGO is recorded in documentary evidence from the twelfth century onwards. It stands a short distance from Lecceto and its name is reminiscent of the now inexistent lake of Verrano. Blessed Agostino Novello lived here at the beginning of the fourteenth century and at that time he was already a well-known figure at the court of Manfredi and then confessor to Pope Nicholas IV. He was nominated general of the Augustinian Order but he refused and retired to S. Leonardo where

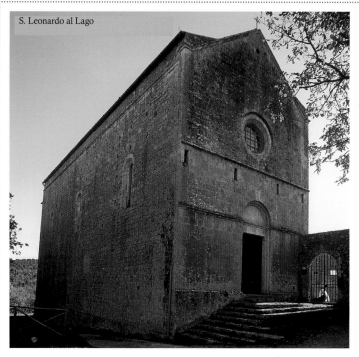

S. Leonardo al Lago

he died in 1309 with immediate calls for his canonisation, as shown by the famous painting on wood by Simone Martini which was once in the Church of S. Agostino and is now in the National Art Gallery. This circumstance obviously attracted attention to the hermitage which led to the construction of the beautiful church in the middle of the century, frescoed for the most part by Lippo Vanni whose Stories of the Virgin in the apse may be his masterpiece. The large fresco of the Crucifixion by Giovanni di Paolo in the chapterhouse, on the other hand, can be traced back to the following century.

◇ 2. CHURCH OF S. GIUSEPPE

This Church stands at the far side of the Prato di S. Agostino. It was built between 1521 and 1653 for the Carpenter's Guild.

THE PALIO

The Church was passed down to the Contrada Capitana dell'Onda (District of the Wave). The inside has a central-plan layout and it is enriched by the presence of precious wooden furnishings, extensive pictorial decoration and a large collection of stucco sculptures. The beautiful sixteenth-century crypt holds the district's museum and a GALLERY OF PLASTER CASTS of the work of **Giovanni Dupré**, a prominent nineteenth-century sculptor who was born in the street leading away from the arch at the corner of the church.

In order to fully appreciate the medieval aspect of the city it is best to choose to follow a itinerary that explores all the more isolated alleyways with their breathtaking panoramas. St. Joseph's arch, next to the church of the same name, is part of the remains of a gateway in the old city walls and it leads to Via Dupré where there is a magnificent view of the Torre del Mangia.

On the 19th March, St. Joseph's Saint's Day, the street comes alive with a market where traditional rice fritters are sold along with the so-called "carrettini di San Giuseppe" ("little carts of St. Joseph"). These are little wooden carts with horses fixed to them that are painted with the colours of the districts and move along on their pine-cone wheels.

From Via Dupré you can turn left into Vicolo del Ponte and after the crossroads with Casato di Sotto proceed into Vicolo di Tone. On the corner between the two streets there is an old road tabernacle with a fifteenth-century wooden shrine. The shrine previously contained a seventeenth-century painting which was damaged then substituted in 1999 with a painting by the master decorator **Cesare Olmastroni**. Vicolo di Tone leads into Via di Città right next to the PALAZZO CHIGI SARACINI.

◇
3 PALAZZO CHIGI SARACINI (♟)

This building was originally the residence of the Ghibelline Marescotti family then it became the property of the Piccolomini family but it is currently known by the name of its last owner, whose passion for music saw it become the premises of the Accademia Musicale Chigiana, an internationally renowned, prestigious Sienese institution. The building's destiny, however, had already taken a precociously modern turn to become a cultural site of public enjoyment in 1806. The then owner Galgano Saracini opened up his art collection to the public after he had renovated the house to transform it into a visual celebration of his family's dynasty.

The courtyard with its crenellated walls, the Loggia with sixteenth-century frescoes, various sculptural portraits set around the sides and the well from another convent all give a sense of different eras and the work done by different people over time. There is further telling evidence of this in the sculpture in the entrance hall depicting Pope Julius III Del Monte, which was done in 1609 as a portrait of Paul V Borghese and then altered when Galgano Saracini bought it to celebrate the family link with the pontiff.

THE CHIGI SARACINI COLLECTION is in the museum on the main floor (open to visitors periodically) and has one of its masterpieces on display immediately in the entrance loggia – the relief by **Donatello** depicting the *Madonna and Child benedictory*. The first room, however, gives a better sense of the remarkable atmosphere and high quality of the works of art on display with the wonderful *St. Martin and the Poor* by **Sassetta**. This painting hangs on the window side of the room and is iconic of the whole collec-

tion, while the *Sorrowful Madonna and St. John* – like the first painting on wood from a painted cross that the monks of St. Martin sawed up in 1820 "to make doors" – are positioned either side of a large mirror. The console table below holds the triptych attributed to the extremely graceful **Master of the Osservanza** and is surrounded by oriental porcelain. A valuable Murano glass lamp hangs in the centre of the room over a rare table painted in gold, a precious work of art from the end of the sixteenth century which, in all likelihood, came from one of the Medici residences

as they had started the fashion for this so-called "Indian" furniture.

The subsequent rooms are all full of furnishings which are quite frequently more important as works of art than the paintings hanging on the walls, even though they boast the signatures of **Sano di Pietro**, **Sodoma**, **Beccafumi** and **Marco Pino**. The most interesting works are the little ivory boxes from the Embriachi workshop, a rare sixteenth-century plate painted on a black background which can probably be attributed to **Rutilio Manetti** and a neoclassic cabinet from a design by **Agostino Fantastici**. The sculptures are also particularly noteworthy as they include archaeological bronze work and gothic reliefs by **Gano di Fazio** and **Giovanni d'Agostino**, an exemplary perspective composition by **Francesco di Giorgio Martini**, sketches by **Beccafumi**, **Bernini** and **Foggini** and finally a large plaster model for the Cathe-

Palazzo Chigi Saracini, decorated vault of the Loggia
Palazzo Chigi Saracini, Inside the "studiolo"
Maestro delle Eroine Chigi, *Cleopatra*, 1513–1515

dral's side door which was made in bronze in 1946 by **Vico Consorti.** The actual exhibition rooms, however, are a particularly integral part of this collection's charm, with their house-museum organisation and their neoclassical pictorial decoration. The decorative work took place at the same time as a restoration project between the end of the eighteenth century and the early nineteenth century and the large neo-Rococo concert room which was inaugurated in 1923 is no less impressive.

◇
4 Palazzo delle Papese

This building almost faces the Palazzo Chigi Saracini and was built in the second half of the fifteenth century for one of Pius II's sisters, Caterina Piccolomini, but just a century later it was associated with both the Pope's sisters and called "Papesse". It was built by **Antonio Federighi** but it is not known if he followed his own design or one by **Bernardo Rossellino**. The building was restored at the beginning of the twentieth century and has long been the local premises of the Bank of Italy. In 1998 it linked its name to a dynamic international centre of contemporary art promoted by the local municipal administration. Proceeding a short distance along Via di Città you come to the Chiasso del Bargello on the right which slopes steeply down to the Piazza del Campo.

 *Retracing your steps…*

To return to the car park after completing itinerary **0** (see pgs. 12–51) you have to leave Piazza del Duomo by Via del Capitano and cross over Piazza della Postierla (ver pág. 87-88) to proceed along Via S. Pietro until Prato di S. Agostino. Continue straight on along Via Mattioli and you will see the entrance to the car park.

The PALAZZO BONSIGNORI, an imposing, fifteenth-century late Gothic building, and the adjacent PALAZZO BRIGIDI PANNOCCHIESCHI stand on the left-hand side of Via S. Pietro. These two buildings are the current home of the National Art Gallery (Pinacoteca Nazionale).

◇ 5 NATIONAL ART GALLERY

The Gallery came under state control in 1930 and originates from the collection of Abbot Giuseppe Ciaccheri, an eighteenth-century Sienese learned man who was also the first librarian – with a lifelong appointment – of the then newly founded Library "BIBLIOTECA DEGLI INTRONATI". This was a prestigious institution which is still based in Via della Sapienza in the University's original nucleus of buildings. Works from dissolved religious institutions and other collections were added to Ciaccheri's, including the group of Flemish paintings from the Spannocchi collection and a series of Sienese sculptures from the fourteenth and fifteenth centuries. The unique slab of marble incised with a *Crucifixion* is one of the particularly noteworthy sculptures. It can be dated to the early fourteenth century and is attributed to **Guccio di Mannaia**, the great goldsmith, engraver of seals and inventor of the translucent glaze technique.

The most important display sections focus on Sienese painting from the thirteenth to the sixteenth centuries but the museum certainly does not lack other works of great interest like, for example, the *Mystical Marriage of St. Catherine* by **Michelino da Besozzo**, which is one of the most well-known paintings from the Lombard international Gothic era. Taking an ideal journey through the fundamental stages of the history of Sienese painting, the *Madonna of St. Bernardine* cannot be missed. It is mentioned in documentary evidence in 1262 and can be attributed to the circle of **Guido da Siena**, the painter who is traditionally thought of as the local artistic school's initial point of reference. The pictorial decoration of a tabernacle with doors comes from the same cultural moment in time and the object itself was probably used as a holder for the relics of Andrea Gallerani, the Blessed Sienese man who died in 1251. He is depicted on the tabernacle in prayer in front of the Cross with the unique iconographic detail of hair tied back with a cord hanging from above. His hair would thus have been pulled if his head had nodded from tiredness during his constant practice of adoration. A small, but certainly not insignificant *Madonna of the Franciscans* by the great protagonist of Sienese art, **Duccio di Buoninsegna**, is kept here and the title of the piece originates from the three little kneeling friars at the feet of the Virgin Mary. Duccio's followers are also well represented, especially with works by **Ugolino di Nerio**, **Segna di Buonaventura** and **Maestro di Città di Castello**. **Simone Martini** was certainly a more well-known figure then as he worked for the Angiò family in Naples, at the Assisi worksite and he also spent a great deal of time at the Papal court at Avignon. Works by Martini on display here include the famous polyptych with

Pietro Lorenzetti, *Carmine Polyptych*

Blessed Agostino Novello and the enchanting *Madonna and Child* from Lucignano d'Arbia, which was only rediscovered at the end of the last century under a later repainting. The examples of work by the leaders of early fourteenth-century Sienese painting are completed by the **Lorenzetti** brothers. Both of them have important works in the collection such as the *Carmine Polyptych* by Pietro – a sublime example of narrative graphic quality, signed and dated 1329 – and the *Annunciation* by Ambrogio, with its simple spatial organisation, signed and dated in 1344. Ambrogio has traditionally been credited with two landscapes, which are extraordinary as lone subjects for that point in time, but these have more recently been attributed with good reason to Sassetta and shifted to a little less than a century later.

Bartolo di Fredi must be mentioned as one of the most high-spirited artists of the late fourteenth century with his crowded and even amusing portrayals. A good example can be seen in the *Adoration of the Magi* whose riding party passes through a town which is easily recognisable as Siena with its Cathe-

dral. The taste for narration, typical of all early Sienese painting becomes even more refined in the *Nativity of the Virgin* by **Paolo di Giovanni Fei**, an obvious enlargement of the one by **Pietro Lorenzetti** in the Museo dell'Opera del Duomo. This trend crossed over into the fifteenth century with artists such as **Martino di Bartolomeo**, **Spinello Aretino**, **Lorenzo Monaco**, **Sano di Pietro** and **Giovanni di Paolo**.

Lorenzo di Pietro known as Vecchietta appeared to be an altogether more versatile artist, as demonstrated by the painted model for a large tabernacle which he himself made in bronze in 1467 and can still be seen today in the Cathedral.

Francesco di Giorgio Martini was an even more multi-talented artist and certainly one of the most important figures of Renaissance Siena. His paintings on display here are a real example of perspective form.

New ideas were brought to Siena in the sixteenth century by the Umbrian **Pin-**

Lorenzo Vecchietta, *Design for a Tabernacle*

Francesco di Giorgio Martini, *Coronation of the Virgin*

toricchio and the Piedmontese artist **Sodoma**, both of whom worked extensively in the city. Their respective works include the *Sacred Family* and *Christ at the Column*. Another superb leader in the new "way" was **Domenico di Pace known as Beccafumi**, whose knowledgeable and extremely personal artistry in playing with contrasts of light is demonstrated here in a large number of important works. Other examples of sixteenth-century work include a *St. Jerome* by **Dürer** dated 1514, a *Child's Bath* by **Lorenzo Lotto** and a remarkable piece almost certainly by **Sofonisba Anguissola**, which represents the artist herself while her portrait is painted by Bernardino Campi. As regards the seventeenth century, other than works by the pride of the local area **Rutilio Manetti**, there is a *Martyrdom of St. Martina* by **Pietro da Cortona** and a *Temptation of St. Francis* by **Jacopo Ligozzi** which is painted in a monochrome style reminiscent of engraving.

◇
6 Church of S. Pietro alle Scale

A flight of steps next to the Art Gallery leads to this church which is also known by the name "in Castelvecchio". It is a thirteenth-century building which was completely transformed between the seventeenth and the eighteenth centuries but it contains an interesting dismantled polyptych ascribed to **Ambrogio Lorenzetti**.

7 Museo dell'Accademia dei Fisiocritici

The entrance to this building is on the right of the Prato di S. Agostino. The Academy of Physiocritics was founded in 1691 and can boast of prestigious former members such as Linnaeus, Volta, Lagrange and Pasteur. Its name was invented from a union of the Greek words for "nature" and "judges" by its founder Pirro Maria Gabbrielli, a professor of theoretical medicine and botany at the local University. The museum is comprised of rich and important palaeontological, mineral, mycological, zoological, ornithological and anatomical collections. Among the wide variety of objects on display some of the must-see curiosities include a meteorite which fell in the Sienese countryside in 1794, a cup made of a coconut which belonged to Napoleon and a collection of birds donated by the politician Bettino Ricasoli, who was also a member of the Academy.

8 Botanical Garden

The entrance to the garden is also on the Prato di S. Agostino, at the top of Via Mattioli. Its foundation in 1588 was linked to the creation of the teaching post of "lector of the Semplici [gardens]" so that future doctors could get to know the plants and their therapeutic qualities. The founder of the Accademia dei Fisiocritici, Pirro Maria Gabbrielli, was particularly interested in the Garden.
Its position in the valley of S. Agostino, protected by the North winds and sloping at 350 to 280 metres above sea level, permitted the outdoor cultivation of

plants which needed varying climates whether hot or alpine. This natural situation is supplemented by the presence of two greenhouses, tepidaria and a lemon-house which contain other botanical varieties, thus making the visit fascinating all year round.

◇ 9 THE TOLOMEI GARDENS

The entrance to this other green area is a slightly further ahead on the other side of the street. These wide open meadows on Valdimontone provide a splendid view over the juncture between the countryside and the city with the spectacular sight of the Basilica dei Servi on the right and the Torre del Mangia on the left. An interesting and unexpected aspect of this secluded urban area is *The Drop*, the monumental sculpture by the English artist **Tony Cragg**, who can be included among the brightest interpreters of contemporary artistic language in the world. (*PANORAMIC VIEW)

Trees and foliage around the walls

4. PORTA S. MARCO

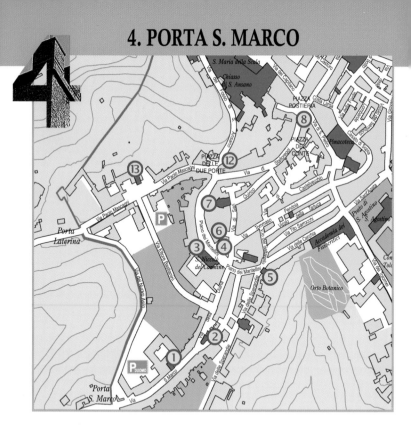

There are plenty of parking possibilities around PORTA SAN MARCO. You can then follow the street of the same name to reach the CONVENT OF S. MARTA (ST. MARTHA).

◇
1 CONVENT OF S. MARTA

This convent has long been dissolved but the church contains an original four-teenth-century frescoed choir including a *Burial of St. Martha* attributed to **Matteo Giovannetti**. There are also fragmentary frescoes with scenes of reclusive life in the internal courtyard and can be traced back to between the fourteenth and fifteenth centuries. On the building opposite, which was once a hospice, there is a painting of the *Christ Crucified with a faithful follower at his feet* by **Ventura Salimbeni** from the early seventeenth century.

◇
2 CHAPEL OF THE MADONNA OF THE ROSARY

Continuing along Via S. Marco you come to the lively eighteenth-century façade of the CHAPEL OF THE MADONNA OF THE ROSARY (CAPPELLA DELLA MADONNA DEL ROSARIO), which impressively marks the fork in the road.

THE PALIO

The chapel has long been deconsecrated and is currently used by the Contrada della Chiocciola (District of the Snail) as a "horse house", the place where the house chosen for the Palio is kept for the three days be-fore the race. This was the district's oratory until 1814 when it moved to SS. Pietro e Paolo.

4

Domenico Beccafumi, *St. Michael banishing the rebellious angels*

The way into the heart of the city from here leads along Via della Diana, the street named after the mythical underground river that the Sienese people searched for pointlessly and the reason why Dante mocked them as "vain individuals" (*Purgatory*, XIII, 150-153). After this street you reach Pian dei Mantellini, a name which derived from the Sienese people's way of referring to the robes of the Carmelites at the convent of S. NICCOLÒ DEL CARMINE.

◇
3 S. NICCOLÒ DEL CARMINE

Externally this building almost blends into the background but inside there are some works of great interest, like a painting on wood and a fresco by **Sodoma** in the Chapel of the Sacrament, and more especially one of **Domenico Beccafumi**'s most famous masterpieces, *St. Michael banishing the rebellious angels*. This work of art has been here since 1535 and is said to have been done by the painter as a "correction" of the first version with the same subject which is currently in the National Art Gallery and defined by Vasari as "confused", even though it has "a very beautiful group of naked figures".

The neoclassical Palazzo Incontri stands just after the Church of the Carmine. It is characterised by white statues in niches, while the sixteenth-century Palazzo Celsi Pollini Neri sits on the other side of Pian dei Mantellini.

◇
4 Palazzo Celsi Pollini Neri
This building sits on the corner of Via di S. Quirico and its beauty is down to **Baldassare Peruzzi**. The Church of SS. Nicolò e Lucia (St. Nicholas and St. Lucy) is at the top of Via S. Quirico on the opposite side of the street where it widens out.

◇
5 Church of SS. Niccolò e Lucia
This church was simply renovated between the sixteenth and seventeenth centuries based on a medieval style and with a bright white interior which holds, among other pieces, interesting works in carved wood. The church comes alive in an extraordinary way on the 13th December for the Saint's Day of their co-patron saint. As the protectress of sight, St. Lucy is the object of widespread popular devotion on this day with people maintaining the tradition of the blessing of the eyes, the distribution of blessed bread and a fair in the surrounding streets where terracotta "campanine" (little bells) are sold, decorated with the colours of the 17 Contrade (Districts) of the city.

> **The Palio**
>
> By going up the Vicolo del Saltarello in front of the church and turning right into Via Tommaso Pendola you will come to the Church of S. Antonio da Padova, Oratory of the Contrada della Tartuca (Turtle).

◇
6 Church known as "delle Carceri di S. Ansano"
Proceeding along Via di S. Quirico you come to the Church of St. Ansanus' Imprisonment. Its name derives from a tradition which states that the Patron

Saint of Siena was kept prisoner in the adjacent tower. Inside there are noteworthy remains of fifteenth-century frescoes from the Sienese school. Between the 1880s and 1890s the INSTITUTE OF DI SANTA TERESA was built next to the church with an oratory characterised by decorations and paintings in line with the purism of the local Academy. Further on, the street opens out to reveal the CHURCH OF SS. QUIRICO E GIULITTA (St. Quiricus and Julitta).

◇
7 CHURCH OF SS. QUIRICO E GIULITTA

This was once the oratory of the Panther, a purpose which is now fulfilled by the Church of the Carmine. Its original medieval appearance was altered between the late sixteenth century and the early seventeenth century and it contains paintings by the leaders of Sienese art of the era, such as **Ventura Salimbeni** and **Francesco Vanni**.

THE PALIO

The MUSEO DELLA CONTRADA (THE DISTRICT MUSEUM) is on the same street and aside from the many banners it has won, including two seventeenth century ones from similar "bufalate" (high-speed buffalo races), it contains a wooden *Madonna* known as *"of the Mandorla"* from **Jacopo della Quercia**'s circle. This work of art has unfortunately been heavily repainted in the past. There is also a painting on canvas depicting the patron *St. John Beheaded*, done by **Antonio Nasini** around 1690 and various other furnishings from the eighteenth and nineteenth centuries.

Via S. Quirico converges on Via di Castelvecchio where you can turn left to reach Via Stalloreggi. On the corner there is a tabernacle where **Sodoma** frescoed a *Piety* commonly known as the *"Madonna of the Crow"*, because this is said to be the place where the death of a crow gave the first sign the plague had spread in 1348. Continuing along Via di Stalloreggi you come to the PIAZZA DELLA POSTIERLA.

◇
8 PIAZZA DELLA POSTIERLA

This is a crossroads between the four main streets of this *terziere* (area) and is therefore commonly known as "the Four Corners". A column with a she-wolf stands here and is representative of this third of the city. The current she-wolf is a recent work by the sculptor **Giuliano Vangi**, while the fifteenth-century work is conserved in Palazzo Pubblico.

The FONTANINA BATTESIMALE (LITTLE BAPTISMAL FOUNTAIN) of the Contrada dell'Aquila (Eagle) also stands in this little square. It was sculpted in 1963 by **Bruno Buracchini**, an artist who had already made a fountain for the Contrada della Tartuca (Tortoise) in Via Tommaso Pendola in 1951. The districts' baptismal rite involves the Prior of the district wetting the children's heads with water from the area's fountain and giving them a handkerchief with the district's colours as a keepsake. The ritual only began to take place 1949 and stems from an idea suggested by Silvio Gigli, the well-known radio broadcaster who always kept strong ties with his birthplace. It is for this reason that various districts have established little fountains especially for the ritual since then, although others use the ancient existing fountains. The Contrada dell'Oca (Goose), for example, uses the historic and magnificent Fonte Branda.

PALAZZO BORGHESI faces onto Piazza della Postierla and its façade was once decorated with mythological scenes painted in chiaroscuro by **Beccafumi**. These decorations have now been lost, just like the ones done by **Sodoma** using the same technique on the nearby *de' Bardi* house. Continuing along Via di Città the
9 PALAZZO DELLE PAPESSE (see p. 77) is on the right and the
10 PALAZZO CHIGI SARACINI (see pgs. 75–77) is on the left. A short distance ahead on the right the Chiasso del Bargello leads down to the Piazza del Campo.

Retracing your steps…
After completing itinerary **0** (see pgs. 12–51) you can leave Piazza del Duomo to go towards the Piazzetta della Selva by going down the stairs in Vicolo S. Sebastiano which lead to the
11 CHURCH OF S. SEBASTIANO IN VALLEPIATTA (see p. 90). Continuing along the Via del Fosso di S. Ansano, which offers a breathtaking glimpse of both the surrounding countryside and the imposing rear façade of S. Maria della Scala, you can reach the PIAZZA DELLE DUE PORTE.

12 PIAZZA DELLE DUE PORTE

This square is called "of the two gates" because of the presence on the left of the arch of the same name which is part of the old city walls from the eleventh century. A noteworthy observation is that there is a painted tabernacle both on the exterior and the interior of the structure. The one on the exterior is one of the oldest road images in the city and depicts a *Madonna and Child* ascribed to a painter from among Duccio's followers in the early fourteenth century. The one on the interior has a sixteenth-century stucco frame which surrounds a *Madonna and Child with St. Catherine* ascribed to **Bartolomeo di David.** The modern CHURCH OF THE CLARISSES faces onto Via Mascagni which starts just outside the gates.

13 CHURCH OF THE CLARISSES

This church contains a *Madonna and Christ enthroned* from the late thirteenth century.
The car park is just ahead on the left.

5. PORTA DI FONTEBRANDA

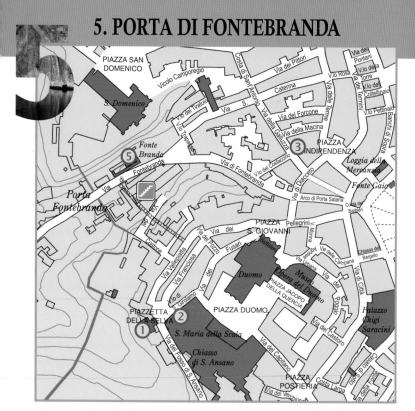

The "Santa Caterina" car park gives easy access to the town through the nearby Porta di Fontebranda. On the right of the gate there is an escalator which goes up to Via Franciosa. From there you turn left to reach the Piazzetta della Selva, where the oratory of the homonymous Contrada (Selva, i.e. Forest) can be seen.

◇ 1 S. Sebastiano in Vallepiatta

The Church of St. Sebastian in Vallepiatta was built by the Weavers' Guild between 1493 and 1550.

The Palio

It has been used as the Contrada della Selva (Forest) since 1818 and the altar holds the venerated image of the *Madonna of the Forest* in stucco and polychrome terracotta. It can be dated to around 1474 and is attributed to **Francesco di Giorgio Martini**, who is also credited with the design of the building. The frescoes which decorate the inside can be dated to between the late sixteenth century and the early seventeenth century and are the work of **Pietro Sorri**, **Giovan Paolo Pisani** and **Raffaello Vanni**, while next to the seventeenth-century wooden *Crucifix* on the right-hand altar there is the *Sorrowful*, painted by **Rutilio Manetti**. The fifteenth-century Crypt houses the district's museum which has the distinctive banner won in the Palio in 1750 on display, while precious liturgical furnishings can still be seen in the sacristy.

The large structure of Santa Maria della Scala backs onto Via del Fosso di S. Ansano, a road which begins at the Piazzetta. From there you can turn directly into the restored Chiasso di S. Ansano.

5

2 CHIASSO DI S. ANSANO

This is a medieval street which was already enclosed in the fourteenth century. It is now an evocative entrance way to begin the visit of the building complex and go up from the inside to reach Piazza del Duomo, thus following itinerary **0** (see pgs. 12–51) backwards.

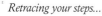

Retracing your steps...
After completing itinerary **0**, which finishes in Piazza del Campo, you can go back towards the car park by following Via Beccheria and continuing along

3 VIA DELLA GALLUZZA

through the most atmospheric medieval area of the city, with its little alleyways characterised by archways linking the sides of the houses. Then you come into Via S. Caterina near

4 ST. CATHERINE'S SANCTUARY (see pgs. 58–60), to finally reach the FONTE BRANDA.

5 FONTE BRANDA

This is the most famous example of a large Gothic Sienese fountain in the city, just inside the gate you came in through. A fountain by this name is mentioned as being in Siena in 1081, but the current crenellated structure can be traced back to 1246. It is characterised by three large acute arches which lead to a covered space entirely filled by a reservoir of water. This place has such fascinating charm that it has also been the object of contemporary art installations. The external decoration is completed by four leonine spouts, the city's coat of arms and a plaque with a quote from the *Divine Comedy*. It is by no means certain that this is the Fonte Branda referred to by Dante (*Hell*, XXX, 78), but in this case tradition triumphs over logic.

6. PORTA OVILE

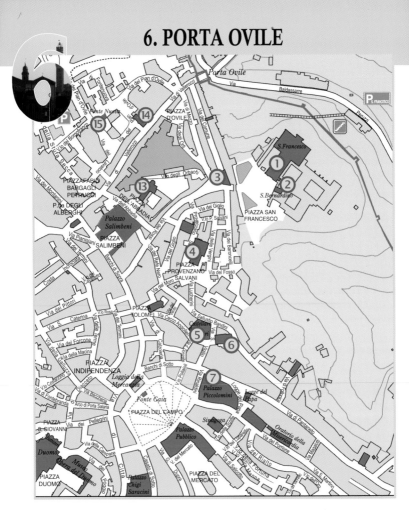

The "San Francesco" car park is just outside the city walls at Porta Ovile and it provides easy access to the city centre thanks to a nearby escalator. This leads up onto Via Peruzzi right to the rear of the CHURCH OF S. FRANCESCO (St. Francis), the first extraordinary stopping point on this itinerary.

◊
1 CHURCH OF S. FRANCESCO

The church's current appearance is the result of several conversion and restoration projects, although we can still form an idea of the façade's original aspect from the painting by **Sano di Pietro** depicting the *St. Bernardine's Sermon in Piazza S. Francesco*

❶

(1444–1450), on display in the Museo dell'Opera del Duomo. There are some equally diverse works of art inside the church including the outstanding frescoes by **Pietro** and **Ambrogio Lorenzetti** which can be traced back to around 1331. These were originally in the convent's Sala Capitolare (Chapterhouse) and the Chiostro (Cloister) but now they are kept in part in the two chapels of the left transept. At the far end of the right transept, on the other hand, there is a fifteenth-century statue of *St. Francis* by **Francesco di Valdambrino.**

A curious occurrence linked to this church has led to the worship of the Sacred Particles there. The consecrated Host was the object of a theft on the 14th August 1730 and it was found three days later miraculously intact. Seeing as the Host was found on the 17th, the event is celebrated on

Ambrogio Lorenzetti, *Martyrdom of the Franciscans at Ceuta*

Sano di Pietro, *St. Bernardine's Sermon in Piazza S. Francesco.* Museo dell'Opera that date each month. The church even has two chapels for the purpose, one in the left transept used in summer and one in the right transept used in the colder months which is decorated on the left-hand wall with a false polyptych frescoed by **Lippo Vanni.**

Beyond the Gate

Basilica of the Osservanza (...)

The Franciscans also had another base in Siena known as the Convent of the Osservanza. It sits on the Colle della Capriola (Capriola Hill) less than two kilometres from the Porta Ovile, so it is easily reachable from the S. Francesco car park by going up Via Peruzzi until the gate itself then following the directions down Via Simone Martini. The name "Osservanza" derives from the return movement to the origins of Franciscanism with St. Bernardine as one of its supporters. The ground where the Saint constructed the first church and adjoining convent was given to him in 1404 by the Hospital of

Basilica of the Osservanza

Sano di Pietro, *St. Bernardine,* 1450 ca. Palazzo Pubblico, Room of the Council

Panorama of Siena from the Basilica of the Osservanza

Santa Maria della Scala, whose oratory of the Order of the Madonna under the Vaults still holds a crucifix in front of which, as tradition has it, Bernardine decided to become a Franciscan.

The current church was rebuilt after the bombardments of January 1944 according to how it would have looked between 1474 and 1490. There are many works by the della Robbia artists inside which were redone to a large extent after the war and painted by **Sano di Pietro**, **Pietro di Giovanni d'Ambrogio**, **Andrea di Bartolo** and **Pietro degli Orioli**. There is also a triptych of the *Madonna with St. Ambrose and St. Jerome* dated in 1436, which is now attributed to the unidentified, refined artist known as the "**Master of the Osservanza**".

In the sacristy there is a splendid *Lamentation of Christ*, a sculptural grouping in polychrome terracotta commissioned for the church's own burial ground by the Magnifico Pandolfo Petrucci, a Lord of the city who was particularly generous to the Bernardinian institution. **Giacomo Cozzarelli**, who is also credited with the design of the church, sculpted the work. Among the interior furnishings the *inlaid pews* by **Antonio di Neri Barili** (1497) are also very interesting.

The Museo Aurelio Castelli has been set up in the adjoining rooms with its glass-enclosed loggia offering a spectacular panorama over Siena. Its name commemorates the exceptional, learned man of the cloth who undertook to collect and preserve works of art at risk of dispersal following the nineteenth-century dissolution of the convents. The museum was inaugurated in 1920 but it has since been repeatedly reorganised.

The convent holds an important collection of illuminated manuscripts that constitute direct proof of the activities of the *scriptorium* established by St. Bernardine. The *wooden crucifix*, once on the church's altar, is also an extremely important piece and the head has remained incredibly expressive in spite of the damage. The bombardments in 1944 actually ripped the sculpture apart and led to the discovery of a scroll the artist had hidden in the knee cavity with the inscription "*Anno domini trecentesimo triginta septe Iesu Cristo per la tua misericordia ti sia raccomandata lanima di lando pieri orafo il quale fabrio questo crocifixo*" (*In anno domini three hundred and thirty seven [1337] for your mercy let the soul of the goldsmith lando pieri be entrusted to you, who made this crucifix*). Besides giving a precise date and attribution to the work, this inscription also tells us a lot about the technical identity and self

regard of artists at the time. In this case Lando di Pietro, the important architect who designed the city's new Cathedral, describes himself as a goldsmith. He does not consider sculpting in wood demeaning yet he does not reveal his name explicitly, only hidden in a prayer, never thinking for a moment it could be read by another human eye. Among the other works of art on display, including many ancient textile vestments, there is a detached fresco of the *Universal Judgement* attributed to **Girolamo di Benevenuto** and a *tombstone* sculpted by **Lorenzo di Pietro known as Vecchietta** for Benvento Piccolomini, archbishop of Benevento. There is also a particularly significant reliquary with the cape of St. Bernardine, a precious silver and gilded copper urn richly decorated with enamel filigrees. The goldsmith **Francesco d'Antonio** completed this work in 1461, probably following an original design by **Giovanni di Turino** who had received the commission in 1446 but died before he could finish it. From the sacristy visitors can go down into the CRYPT, the former burial area of the Petrucci family but as a result of wartime incidents only the elegant sixteenth-century monument for Celia Petrucci remains intact. The tombs of the artists Francesco di Giorgio Martini, Giacomo Cozzarelli and Pietro degli Orioli lay in the adjacent area known as the CRIPTA GRANDE (LARGE CRYPT). St. Bernardine's cell has been reconstructed at the end of the convent's entrance corridor, while another splendid panorama over Siena awaits visitors further ahead from the rear balcony. (*PANORAMIC VIEW)

◇
2 ORATORY OF THE COMPANY OF ST. BERNARDINE

The ORATORIO DELLA COMPAGNIA DI S. BERNARDINO faces onto the Piazza di S. Francesco on the right-hand side in relation to the church and the convent. It is well recognisable by the symbol of the large rayed circle with the monogram of Christ which stands out on the simple brickwork façade.
The building currently houses the MUSEO DIOCESANO.

Oratory of the Company of
St. Bernardine, inside the
Superior Oratory

The most famous work in the museum is perhaps the *Madonna of the Milk* painted by **Ambrogio Lorenzetti** in the early 1320s which comes from the Augustinian Hermitage of Lecceto. Other works include more paintings by **Ambrogio** and **Pietro Lorenzetti**, anonymous thirteenth-century artists like the **Maestro di Tressa**, fourteenth-century Sienese artists like **Segna di Bonaventura**, the so-called **Maestro d'Ovile (Bartolomeo Bulgarini)**, **Lippo Vanni** and **Taddeo di Bartolo**. Then there are paintings by fifteenth-century artists like the **Master of the Osservanza**, **Sano di Pietro**, **Giovanni di Paolo**, **Vecchietta**, **Domenico di Niccolò dei Cori**, **Benvenuto di Giovanni** and **Matteo di Giovanni** and sixteenth-century artists like **Sodoma**, **Domenico Beccafumi** and **Ventura Salimbeni**. Artists from the seventeenth century include **Rutilio Manetti** and **Bernardino Mei**. The UPPER ORATORY or the CHAPEL OF ST. MARY OF THE ANGELS is particularly interesting. The Oratory's name comes from the brotherhood the building originally belonged to and it still has all its original ornamentation. The wooden ceiling was commissioned in 1496 to **Ventura di ser Giuliano di Tura**, who also made the friezes around the cycle of paintings *Stories of the Virgin* by **Sodoma**, **Girolamo del Pacchia** and **Domenico Beccafumi**.

In the penultimate room of the museum there is a more intriguing work on display: a fifteenth-century copy of the famous *Annunciation* by **Simone Martini** which is currently at the Uffizi Gallery in Florence even though it was made in 1333 for Siena Cathedral. The copy was done by **Matteo di Giovanni** for the Church of S. Pietro a Ovile.

THE PALIO

Upon leaving Piazza S. Francesco you can go into Vicolo degli Olbrachi where the ancient FOUNTAIN OF ST. FRANCIS comes into view. The Contrada del Bruco (District of the Caterpillar) use this fountain for their baptism rites and their "horse house" also stands in this little street, the place where the horse chosen by a draw is kept for the three days prior to the race.

◇
3 CHURCH OF S. ELISABETTA DELLA VISITAZIONE

Leaving Piazza S. Francesco along Via de' Rossi you come to this nineteenth-century church with a neo sixteenth-century interior which offers a rare glimpse of the work of female artists. **Luisa Mussini**, daughter of **Luigi** and wife of **Alessandro Franchi** oversaw all the pictorial decorations, while **Alfonsina Marinelli**, daughter of **Gaetano** collaborated on the project along with **Giuseppe Catani-Chiti**.

◇
4 BASILICA OF S. MARIA A PROVENZANO

The BASILICA OF ST. MARY IN PROVENZANO can be reached by turning left into Via Provenzano Salvani.

Building work on this important local religious hub began in 1595 and it was consecrated in 1611 to accommodate a miraculous *Bust of the Virgin*. This bust was formerly on the façade of a house near the destroyed Mansion of the

Provenzano Salvani family, who led the Sienese people to victory against the Florentines in the Battle of Montaperti in 1260.

The miracle happened on the 2nd July 1594 when the terracotta image – which was said to have been part of a *Piety* placed there by St. Catherine – defended itself from the insults of a soldier. People took this as a sign of the protection of the Virgin from the city's occupiers and began to celebrate the anniversary with a Palio. The race was officially organised by the municipality in 1656 and even now precedes the one held in honour of Our Lady of the Assumption.

The building was designed by **Flaminio Del Turco** based on the principles of the Counter-Reformation. This architect also conceived the magnificent High Altar which can be traced back to the second half of the fifteenth century and bears the venerated terracotta bust. The altar sits next to the *Figures in silver of Sienese saints Catherine and Bernardine*, a seventeenth-century work by the brothers **Francesco** and **Giovanni Antonio Mazzuoli**.

THE PALIO

The CHURCH OF THE SUFFRAGIO (Church of the Suffrage) is in the crypt of the Collegiate Church of Provenzano and it has been the oratory of the Contrada della Giraffa (Giraffe) since 1686 when they were welcomed there by the homonymous confraternity. The Opera of Provenzano also let the district use the adjacent rooms to set up a museum with the banners from the Palio.

◇
5 CASTELLARE DEGLI UGURGIERI

Upon leaving the Church you take a left turn at the end of the square into Via Lucherini and then go left again to follow Via Sallustio Bandini, a street which still maintains its thirteenth-century appearance. Next, you turn right into Via S. Viglio and go along Vicolo del Castellare to reach this rare example of an original, medieval urban castle.

THE PALIO

The new CHURCH OF S. ANTONIO DA PADOVA (St. Anthony of Padua) was consecrated in 1945 in the courtyard of the castle. It was constructed by order of the Contrada della Civetta's (District of the Owl's) own patron and their museum is housed in the castle as well. It contains banners won in the Palio, precious articles for worship and a set of old, *Sienese majolica* objects found in a well in 1981.

◇
6 CHURCH OF S. VIGILIO

Going back onto Via S. Vigilio you can see a Church which has the same name as the street. It is strongly characterised by the Jesuits who lived there between 1561 and 1773 and inside it has various sculptures and a wooden ceiling with fifteen paintings on canvases by **Raffaello Vanni** depicting the

whole of the *Universal Judgement*. Moving on until the crossroads with Banchi di Sotto the extremely distinct PALAZZO PICCOLOMINI D'ARAGONA is right in front of you.

◇ 7 PALAZZO PICCOLOMINI D'ARAGONA

You then go along Via Rinaldi which leads to Piazza del Campo. This elegant example of Renaissance construction looks over Banchi di Sotto. Pope Pius II's nephews, Giacomo and Andrea Piccolomini Todeschini, had it built and in order to have a "well-proportioned and magnificent [Palazzo] in all its dimensions", they obtained permission from the "Ufficiali dell'Ornato" to occupy a part of the public ground on the Campo. Building work began

in 1469 perhaps from a design by *Bernardo Rossellino* under the direction of the Sienese **Pier Paolo del Porcina**, while **Marrina** handled the decorative ornamentation.

The ARCHIVIO DI STATO (STATE ARCHIVES) have been kept here since their foundation in 1858 when the town was still under the Grand Ducal government of Tuscany.

The institution also has a museum where there is a permanent collection of "Biccherna" tablets, paintings which were originally used as bindings for the registers of the financial magistrature known by the same name. The oldest tablet depicts the *Camarlingo of St. Galgano seated at his table*. It can be traced back to 1258 and marks the beginning of an incredible sequence of signed and dated works which document a rare aspect of civic painting and Sienese art history as a whole with people like **Ambrogio Lorenzetti**, **Lorenzo Vecchietta**, **Francesco di Giorgio Martini** and other equally interesting artists. Similar tablets were subsequently commissioned by various magistratures of the Municipality and by other civic bodies, and in the fifteenth century they

Francesco di Giorgio Martini and fiduciary of Francesco, "Biccherna" with *The Virgin Mary protecting Siena during the earthquakes*, 1467

Sano di Pietro, "Biccherna" with *The Camarlingo washing his hands. The Virgin Mary protecting Siena*, 1451

became actual paintings. Besides the "Biccherne" – which are meaningfully displayed in their element as archive documents, hence their position partly surrounded by shelves and cupboards with other records – the museum also has other precious documents including historical parchments from the year 735, highly coloured illuminated manuscripts, the testament of Giovanni Boccaccio, documents associated with St. Catherine and St. Bernardine and a lot of pieces linked to the Palio races.

Retracing your steps…

After completing itinerary **0** (see pgs. 12–51) you can go back to Porta Ovile by leaving Piazza del Duomo along Via Capitano until

8 PIAZZA POSTIERLA (see pgs. 87–88) and then turn left into Via di Città, where you can see

9 PALAZZO DELLE PAPESSE (see p. 77),

10 PALAZZO CHIGI SARACINI (see pgs. 75-77) and the

11 LOGGIA DELLA MERCANZIA (see p. 71). Once you reach this Loggia, at the crossroads known as the Croce del Travaglio, you can go up Banchi di Sopra with the easily identifiable medieval structure of the TORRE DELL'ARTE DELLA LANA (TOWER OF THE WOOL MANUFACTURERS' GUILD) at the top of the street. This tower has the guild's coats of arms clearly visible over the typical Sienese arches which currently frame a shop window. Further ahead on the right you come to the

12 PIAZZA TOLOMEI (see p. 70) followed shortly after on the same side of the street by the arch of Via dei Rossi. Under this arch you turn to reach Via dell'Abbadia which leads to the

13 CHURCH OF S. DONATO

This Church was originally an abbey for the friars of Vallombrosa. Inside there are fragmentary late thirteenth-century frescoes and paintings by **Antonio Nasini** (1693), **Giovan Battista Sorbi** (1730) and **Luigi Ademollo** (1794).

The adjacent ORATORY OF S. MICHELE (St. Michael) is currently a cinematographic projection room but it also still contains sixteenth and seventeenth-century frescoes. From here you come into Via di Vallerozzi which leads straight to the original fourteenth-century Porta Ovile and the ensuing car park.

14 ORATORY OF S. ROCCO

The ORATORY OF ST. ROCCO stands in Via Vallerozzi. It has a sixteenth-century structure with a simple and well-proportioned brickwork exterior as opposed to a fully frescoed interior, done in the seventeenth century by Sienese artists like **Rutilio Manetti** who completed a part of the *Stories of St. Rocco*.

THE PALIO

This oratory has belonged to the Contrada della Lupa (District of the She-Wolf) since 1789. In the district's museum underneath there is an altar piece with the *Apparition of the Madonna before St. Rocco*, signed in 1603 by **Ventura Salimbeni**.

---

15 FONTE NUOVA

Pian d'Ovile opens out behind the Church of S. Rocco with a magnificent, partly ruined fountain. It was built between 1295 and 1303 to provide the heart of the growing manufacturing area directly with water. The commission which decided to carry out the work included **Giovanni Pisano** and **Duccio di Buoninsegna**, while the name of **Camaino di Crescentino**, father of the famous sculptor **Tino di Camaino**, is recorded among the constructors.

7. PORTA ROMANA

◇
1 Porta Romana

The tourist buses have a pick up/drop off point inside the gate where there is also a car park. The imposing gate can be traced back to 1327 and used to have pictorial decoration, including an intrados of a *Glory of musician angels* by **Sassetta**. By going along Via Roma you will then come to the Church of Santuccio on the right.

◇
2 Church of Santuccio

This is the only complete remaining part of the ex-convent of S. Maria degli Angeli and inside there are various paintings by Sienese artists from the early seventeenth century. The Museo della Società delle Pie Disposizioni is in what used to be the church's sacristy. This laical society's historical premises are in Santa Maria della Scala. Among the works on display – including paintings by various Sienese masters from the thirteenth to the twentieth centuries – there is a particularly interesting triptych-reliquary in gilded glass and graffito from a design by **Lippo Vanni**. There is also a painted cross from **Duccio di Buoninsegna**'s circle, a lunette with St. Catherine bringing Pope Gregory XI back to Rome by **Girolamo di Benvenuto**, a *Sacred Family* by **Sodoma** and two biers painted by **Guidoccio Cozzarelli**, one of which is dated 1494.

◇
3 Church of S. Leonardo

This Church can be seen as you go up Via di Val di Montone. It was renovated based on a project by **Giovanni Michelucci** to hold a part of the homonymous district's museum as their oratory stands just above in the Company of the SS. Trinità (Holy Trinity).

◇
4 Company of the SS. Trinità

The interior of this building with its closely interwoven combination of paintings and ornamental sculpting represents a brilliant affirmation of the decorative awareness of Sienese art during the latter sixteenth century. The oratory is set between the apse and the left transept of the Church of S. Maria de' Servi.

◇
5 Church of S. Maria de' Servi (✋)

This church stands at the top of flight of steps from which there is a spectacular view over the city. The building was originally built in the thirteenth century and repeatedly enlarged over the following two centuries. Its external architectural appearance was modified by all these projects culminating

Coppo di Marcovaldo,
*Madonna of the Pilgrim's
Staff*

in the destructive restoration of 1925 but inside it
has a series of important works. One of the most
well-known is certainly the *Madonna of the Pilgrim's Staff* by **Coppo di Marcovaldo**, a Floren-

tine painter imprisoned by the Sienese after the battle of Montaperti and he is said to have paid his own ransom with this painting, signed 1261. Among the other artistic works here, the most remarkable ones are the early fourteenth-century frescoes traditionally attributed to **Pietro Lorenzetti** but in actual fact they can be ascribed to **Niccolò di Segna**. These frescoes are in the two chapels at the sides of the presbytery with the *Slaughter of the Innocents* in the second one on the right and *Herod's Banquet* and the *Passing away of St. John the Evangelist* in the second on the left. Both the chapels also have ancient altar tables by **Lippo Memmi** and **Taddeo di Bartolo**. A large painted cross attributed to **Niccolò di Segna** hangs at the far end of the right transept and underneath there is an altar with the venerated remains of Blessed Francesco Patrizi, the most well-loved Servite of Siena known locally as "Francesco Tarlato" ("Worm-Eaten Francesco") because of the state of his body.

Noteworthy pieces among the later works of art include the *Madonna of Mercy* by **Giovanni di Paolo**, dated 1431 and characterised by a vestment with splendid embroidery, a *Slaughter of the Innocents* by **Matteo di Giovanni** dated 1491 and a *Nativity of Mary* by **Rutilio Manetti**, a masterpiece of light effects which can be dated to around 1625.

By going along Via dei Servi you can reach the CHURCH OF S. GIROLAMO (St. Jerome).

◇
6 CHURCH OF S. GIROLAMO

Like the adjacent convent this church holds various works of art including some fifteenth-century frescoes in the ex-cloister by **Bernardino Fungai** and **Fra Giuliano da Firenze** belonging to the order of the Jesuits which occupied the convent at the time. Turning left into Via di Salicotto you arrive in the area of the city where the Jews were confined in 1570 and the GHETTO was still known locally as the "serraglio" (seraglio) in the nineteenth century. The area underwent a substantial renovation from 1929 onwards but the urban structure is still partly made up of narrow alleyways and flights of steps, particularly the area between Via di Salicotto and Vicolo delle Scale. Going back up Vicolo della Fortuna you arrive in front of the SYNAGOGUE.

◇
7 SYNAGOGUE

Built in 1786 this is one of the oldest remaining Synagogues in Tuscany. It was designed by **Zanobi del Rosso**, architect of the Royal Factories of the Grand Duchy, and completed by his son **Giuseppe**. It has a bright interior focused around *Aaron* and the cupboard containing the Scrolls of the Law is on the far wall. The furnishings for rites are also very interesting including the so-called *Seats of Elijah* used for circumcisions.

The CHURCH OF S. GIACOMO, the oratory of the Contrada della Torre (District of the Tower) stands in the Salicotto area. It was constructed between 1532 and 1536 to celebrate the victory over the Florentines, who were supported by the Papal army. The Sienese won this battle on the 25th July 1526, the Saint's Day of St. James. Inside there are two paintings on canvas by **Rutilio Manetti**, while the adjacent museum contains a *Way to Calvary* thought to be one of **Sodoma**'s last works.

Following Vicolo delle Scotte to the right, looking at the Synagogue's façade, you come to the side of the Church of S. Martino which is preceded by the ORATORY OF MERCY (ORATORIO DELLA MISERICORDIA).

◇
8 ORATORY OF MERCY

This Oratory is the result of a nineteenth-century unification of two pre-existing buildings but it still contains a well-proportioned, sixteenth-century altar-piece by **Girolamo del Pacchia** as well as works by the leading Sienese artists at the turn of the sixteenth and seventeenth centuries such as **Rutilio Manetti**, **Pietro Sorri**, **Francesco Vanni** and **Alessandro Casolani**. On the 17th January, the Saint's Day of St. Anthony Abbot, feedstuff and animals are blessed in the church, of which the reclusive Saint is protector.

◇
9 CHURCH OF S. MARTINO

This *terziere* (area) of Siena is named after this Church so in all likelihood it was already in existence in the eighth century. It was renovated in the fourteenth century, restored during the sixteenth century and then given a new façade in the following century. Work on the bell tower, however, only came to an end in 1738. Inside there are paintings by **Domenico Beccafumi**, **Guido Reni** and **Guercino** and the High Altar with its ciborium resting on clouds held up by angels is spectacular. It was made by **Giuseppe** and **Giovanni Antonio Mazzuoli** who, along with other members of the same family of artists, were responsible for a large part of the sculptural ornamentation during the remodelling of the church towards the end of the sixteenth century.

◇◇
10 LOGGE DEL PAPA

This loggia stands very near the church. It was commissioned by Pius II to Antonio Federighi in 1462. The elegant round arches are crowned by a large dedicatory epistle embodying classic rhythm and handwriting. These inscriptions are the most obvious Renaissance addition to the fabric of Siena. Moving on into Via del Porrione you arrive directly into Piazza del Campo.

7

⑩

Retracing your steps...
After completing itinerary **0** (see pgs. 12–51) you can return towards Porta Romana by going along Via di Pantaneto and at the top of this street you make a brief diversion to the left into Via di Follonica to discover S. GIOVANNINO DELLA STAFFA.

THE PALIO

◇◇ 11 S. GIOVANNINO DELLA STAFFA

The Oratory of the Contrada del Leocorno (District of the Unicorn) is a building of Roman origin which appears before us today in the form it acquired in the middle of the sixteenth century. Inside there is a series of thirteen paintings on canvas with *Stories of the life of the Baptist* done between 1599 and 1649 by the masters of Sienese painting at the time such as **Rutilio Manetti**, **Bernardino Mei**, **Astolfo Petrazzi** and **Raffaello Vanni**.

◇◇ 12 CHURCH OF S. GIORGIO

The CHURCH OF S. GIORGIO (St. George) stands back on Via di Pantaneto. The building has a lively, early seventeenth-century façade, although it still has the bell tower made after the battle of Montaperti in honour of the Holy warrior. According to traditions it has thirty-eight windows which commemorate the same number of military campaigns fought against the Florentines by the city. Inside the church on the counter-façade there is a funerary monument of the painter **Francesco Vanni**.

Francesco Vanni's funerary monument is inside the church on the counter-façade and a painting on canvas by the artist depicting the *Crucifixion with Father Matteo Guerra* is on the left-hand wall.

◇◇ 13 CHURCH OF S. SPIRITO

The CHURCH OF THE HOLY SPIRIT can be seen by making a brief detour to the left into Via dei Pispini. It has a Renaissance appearance as it was renovated between the late fifteenth century and the early sixteenth century just after it had been entrusted to the Dominicans. This work took place thanks to the generous donation of the then lord of the city Pandolfo Petrucci. Among the many works of art inside the church, the least commonplace include a crib in polychrome terracotta (1504) by **Ambrogio della Robbia**, a Dominican who belonged to the famous family of masters of this technique, and a painting by **Sodoma** depicting *Santiago Matamoros* [or rather St. Jacob defeating the Moorish], an unusual subject in Italy but typical of Spanish religious observance. In actual fact the Spanish commissioned the work, as the name of the chapel it is kept in reminds us.

If you follow Via dei Pispini you reach the magnificent Gate of the same name. It is a thirteenth-century structure which takes its name from the "pispinelli", that is to say the spouts that water gushes from in the nearby sixteenth-century fountain.

> **THE PALIO**
>
> The ORATORY OF S. GAETANO DI THIENE (St. Cajetan of Thiene) stands in Via dei Pispini where it meets Via dell'Oliviera. It was built at the end of the seventeenth century by the Nobile Contrada del Nicchio (District of the Seashell) and on the façade there is a venerated image in a stucco niche of the *Madonna of the Pitchfork*, an early sixteenth-century painting which has now been substituted by a copy. From the inside of the Oratory, frescoed by **Giuseppe Nicola Nasini** and his son **Apollonio**, you can gain access to the district's museum. Besides the banners from the Palio it contains other precious pieces and works in gold.

◇◇ 14 S. RAIMONDO AL REFUGIO

This church can be reached by going back along Via dell'Oliviera and turning left into Via Fiera Vecchia. It was commissioned by Aurelio Chigi who had transformed the nearby Palazzo di S. Galgano into a refuge for abandoned girls. The church was completed under Pope Alessandro VII Chigi and in line with this Pope's urban vision of architecture, famously demonstrated by the colonnade he commissioned from **Bernini** in Piazza S. Pietro in Rome, he asked the local architect **Benedetto Giovanelli Orlandi** to do both the church's façade and the layout of the short street leading up to it. The architect conceived the street with two simple symmetrical viewpoints which "invite" the eye towards the sacred building, as you can see by looking at the whole scene from Via Roma before going along it to the left to reach the car park.

SIENESE COOKING

SIENA AT THE TABLE

Strolling through Siena means touching with your hand the Middle Ages, when the city reached its peak of splendour. This is one of the most particular places in the whole region. Visited every year by thousands of tourists, who flock here twice a year especially (on July 2 and August 16), it is literally packed with people come to watch the Palio, the ancient horse race that has been run for centuries and that involves the citizens all year round, not only for its organization and preparation, but also in the joyous banquets held in the streets as part of the festivities accompanying the event. The menus on these occasions are reserved to gourmets with hearty appetites, since they consist of dishes using every part of the pig, the interior organs of lamb and chickens, and so on. An important university centre, declared by Unesco *patrimonio dell'umanità*, Siena was a crossroads of thoroughfares and trade, as well as a major stopping place on the Via Francigena on the journey to Rome, offering never-failing welcome and hospitality to travellers and pilgrims. Today as then, its taverns and restaurants offer those who stop a triumph of flavours linked to the dishes of old tradition.

Here 'you eat well and you drink well' in a fusion of tastes and lovely views that open the heart and the belly. The territory of Siena is a succession of breathtaking views amidst cypress trees, olive groves, distant parish churches, castles and rows of grapevines marching over the hills. Here even a simple snack of bread, salami and cheese, either "marzolino" or pecorino – outstanding those of the Crete Senesi, and that of Pienza in particular – assumes another significance if we pause to savour it before the vast green countryside and the towns clinging to the gentle hills of the Crete and of Chianti, emblems of Tuscany itself the world over: Buonconvento, Montepulciano, S. Quirico d'Orcia, Asciano, Monteriggioni, Pienza, Castelnuovo Berardenga, S. Gimignano and Castellina in Chianti, are only some of the marvellous localities to be seen, without forgetting the natural thermal baths of Chianciano, Rapolano, Bagno Vignoni and S. Casciano dei Bagni. Within the city of Siena are places deemed real temples to the ancient culinary tradition, where delicacies from all ages can still be found.

Sienese cuisine retains echoes of Medieval and Renaissance splendour, when banquets were based on meat and game highly flavoured with the spices – the most commonly used, still today, being cinnamon, ginger, saffron, cloves and estragon – that arrived from distant lands, thanks to the city's merchants; while the more humble people found satisfaction in wild herbs picked in the fields and stale bread used for soups. Siena underwent long domination by Florence, which left an imprint on its cooking as well. It should also be remembered, however, that the most famous cooks at the Medici court came from Siena and it was very probably they who created dishes that were to become world-famous such as duck with sweet orange sauce, which then evolved into the better-known **anatra all'arancia** and the sweet called **zuppa del Duca** made of little cakes soaked in liqueur and covered with cream. But although Sienese cooking does not differ highly from that of Florence and despite the fact that it must satisfy the requisites of tourists, it manages to find a good compromise with innovation, while keeping its tradition vitally alive. Still today there remains the customary roasted and grilled meat, as well as stewed game, dressed with special sauces such as **lepre in dolceforte**, but also meat that is boiled as in **stiracchio** or stewed as in **scottiglia**. And here too it is easy to find steaks from cattle of the Chianina breed.

Another dish coming from the recipes of the people is **ginestrata**, a spiced soup that is a real pick-me-up made with eggs, stock and Vin Santo; and then there is **cipollata**.

Only in the last few years has one of the most ancient breeds of pig, already known in the Middle Ages, been rediscovered. This is the breed called **cinta senese**, very special pigs whose name derives from the distinctive light-coloured band (the *cinta*, or belt) that runs around the animal's body. Living in a semi-wild state, these pigs feed on acorns, cereals, truffles and roots, which give their flesh flavour and fragrance. Excellent in fact are the prosciutto, salami, finocchiona and capocollo, as well as the **buristo**, from the cinta senese. This kind of charcuterie – some of which is found in other parts of Tuscany too – where it is also called **mallegato** and is enriched with other ingredients, as for instance in Pistoia with pine nuts and raisins – originated here in the 18th century, derived from the German würstel, to which the Sienese added spices. Recently reintroduced is the cultivation of **zafferano** (saffron) at S. Gimignano, grown there in the Middle Ages and so precious that it was also used to dye fabrics, in artists' paints, and in medicine, and even as a coin of exchange in trading. In the kitchen it is used in preparing sauces and creams for first courses such as **pici**, the pasta in the shape of long spaghetti found also at Grosseto, and even to flavour bread and the flat loaves called "schiacciata". In late October, the "Giallo come l'Oro" (Yellow as Gold) fair is held in the town, with the sampling of typical dishes.

Many are the sweets made for various occasions, such as **schiacciata di Pasqua** and **pan co' Santi** for All Saints' Day, although the best known are the Christmas ones such as **panforte**, **panpepato**, **ricciarelli**, and **cavallucci** exported all over the world, without forgetting such everyday treats as the ancient **torta dei medici** – meaning doctors, and not the famous Florentine family – which was prescribed as an invigorating tonic, made of spinach, honey, apples, almonds and spices; or **copate**, crisp delights containing honey and dried fruit. This part of the region also produces excellent wines, starting from the famous **Brunello di Montalcino**, ranging through **Chianti dei Colli Senesi**, **Vernaccia di S. Gimignano** and ending with the more recent **S. Antimo**.

GLOSSARY

Starters, snacks, savory pies and luncheon dishes

Ciancinfrincola – A tasty speciality whose curious name in dialect indicates something mingled in confusion. It is, in fact, a kind of sauce made of scrambled eggs sautéed with olive oil, garlic, black pepper or hot red pepper and a few tomatoes. It is ideal for spreading on slices of toasted bread.

Crostini bianchi – Rounds of bread with butter, cheese and trifola, or better still, white truffles. It originated in San Gimignano.

Crostini di milza e fegato – A classic Tuscan starter made of chicken liver and veal spleen cooked in wine, blended and spread on rounds of bread. The version in which the bread is first dampened with dry Vin Santo is used.

Fettunta con pecorino di Pienza – The traditional slice of toasted Tuscan bread rubbed with garlic, dressed with olive oil and accompanied by slices of one of the world's oldest and most famous pecorino cheeses. A very simple but remarkably satisfying snack.

Pasta and soups

Brodo con le cicche – A farmers' soup made with chicken stock in which the interior organs and chicken livers are cooked.
Cipollata – An onion soup flavoured with lard and a hambone, known around Florence as **carabaccia**.
Ginestrata – A soup made of eggs, chicken stock, spices and Vin Santo. It has a curious history, being traditionally offered by a mother-in-law to her daughter-in-law when she entered her new home to spend her wedding night.

Pappardelle con la lepre – A classic of Tuscan cooking, but which here as in the Arezzo area finds its ideal scenario, made of very fresh game and just-made pasta in the form of "pappardelle".
Pici – In contesting the origin of this particular type of pasta (*see photo p. 200*) with the nearby town of Grosseto, the Sienese have prepared unusual dressings, such as that of zucchini and saffron, in addition to classic sauces such as those made of meat, sausage or "all'aglione" with abundant garlic and tomatoes.
Stiracchio – A tasty dish made with leftover boiled meat, which is floured and sautéed, then plunged in a sauce of tomatoes and wine. It is served with pepper and a lot of bread.

Strisce e ceci – A richer version of the classic pasta and chick peas, here re-interpreted with partially puréed chick peas dressed with a savoury sauce of tomatoes, onions and garlic in which the "strisce" are cooked. The "strisce" are like tagliatelle but wider and more irregular in shape.

Zuppa senese di fagioli – Slices of stale bread are toasted, dressed with a few drops of olive oil and dusted with grated pecorino. A broth of Cannellini beans, flavoured with olive oil, garlic and pepper, is poured over them.

Meat, fish, and side dishes

Arrosto morto – A dish influenced by Florentine cuisine, made of meat cooked simply with olive oil, garlic and some aromatic herbs.

Fegatelli di maiale alla senese – A very savoury dish made of pork liver covered in pork membranes, flavoured with lard, fennel seeds and lemon rind, and cooked in the oven. The dish is common to other parts of the region as well, with the variation of being cooked on skewers with bay leaves and orange rind, or as is customary in Prato, stewed in a pan with aromatic herbs. It is frequently found as an ingredient of **spiedino alla senese** along with other meats, such as sausage and loin of pork, or as "uccellini" alternating with slices of toasted bread and bay leaves.

Lepre in dolceforte – One of the dishes inherited from the splendours of the Renaissance, consisting of hare that has been hung for a long time, dressed with a particular sweet-and-salty sauce containing onions, prosciutto, carrots, unsweetened chocolate, pine nuts, candied fruit and sugar. A curious and unusual combination, but a real must to be sampled in a local restaurant.

Scottiglia or **Buglione** – A stew made with various kinds of meat (chicken, rabbit, veal, pork, etc.) which are first sautéed and then cooked in a sauce of tomatoes, hot red pepper and red wine. This is a dish typical of the shepherds who brought their flocks from Casentino to the Maremma to graze. Different versions of this dish exist today because it was made with the meat available at the moment.

Cakes, pies, cookies and liqueurs

Cavallucci – Cookies almost round in shape, ranging from soft to hard in consistency, made with walnuts, candied fruits, flour, honey, spices and wine, served with a glass of Vin Santo or Passito in which to dip them. Of very ancient origin, their name derives from the stable boys who took care of the horses at post stations, who consumed them in large quantities, also because they keep for weeks at a time.

Ciambellino – One of the many existing versions of these cookies of humble Tuscan tradition is the one in which they are made of fried bread dough and coated with sugar, typical of Carnival time in Siena.

Copate – A sweet of ancient Arab origin, from which derives its name, formed of two wafers with a crunchy filling of almonds or walnuts and honey, flavoured with anise. They are found in two versions: white (with almonds, honey and egg whites) and black (with finely chopped dried fruit, honey and cocoa).

Goglioli – A tastier version of the chestnuts "bruciate" over burning coals, in which they are sprinkled with Chianti red wine when almost done and are covered with a clean cloth before being eaten. Some cooks like to peel them and plunge them in a glass of red wine.

Pan co' Santi – This is a soft, sweet loaf from the humble foods tradition, prepared especially for the time around All Saints' Day, containing walnuts, raisins, flour and sugar and usually accompanied by the new wine taken from the wine barrels in early November.

Panforte – The classic version is a round, hard cake made of flour, almonds,

spices, candied fruit and honey, resting on a base of thin wafers and sprinkled with cocoa. In the past it was made with sweet fruit – grapes, figs and apples – baked in the oven, to which flour was then added to form a dough. It did not last for a long time, and after a few days could take on an acid taste, and was called in fact "forte" (strong). There is also a more recent version containing chocolate.

Panforte Margherita or **Bianco** – This is a sweeter, more delicate version of the cake described above, from which it differs in containing more spices, candied citron instead of melon, and in being enriched with vanilla extract and powdered sugar sprinkled on top. It was created in 1879 in honour of Queen Margherita di Savoia, who came to Siena to see the Palio.

Panpepato – This sweet cake has the same basic ingredients as panforte, but with the addition of ground black pepper and sometimes of cocoa as well, making it truly special.

Its origin is lost in time, but it is known to have been baked for Christmas already in the 16th century. But its history is also linked to one of the many sieges undergone by the city. It is said that a nun invented it, based on a "focaccia" with fruit similar to "panforte", a new sweet designed to stimulate the energy of the citizens by the addition of ginger, candied fruit and pepper.

Pinolata – A very simple Easter sweet made of flour, sugar, butter, eggs and pine nuts, flavoured with lemon or orange, made either with or without cream.

Ricciarelli – One of the world's most famous Christmas cookies, made of marzipan, eggs, and honey flavoured with vanilla. They have a characteristic diamond shape, with a cracked surface dusted with powdered sugar and are very soft. There also exists a version lightly coated in chocolate. Their origin dates from the time of the Crusades, when they were introduced into Siena by a crusader called Ricciardetto, for whom they were then named, who had first tasted them in the Holy Land.

Schiacciata di Pasqua – A soft, fluffy twice-risen cake traditionally served at Easter, made of flour, sugar and eggs flavoured with mint liqueur, Vin Santo and orange juice. Its name derives from the custom of crushing eggs at the end of Lent.

Tegole di Montalcino – Cookies containing the famous wine with the addition of spices, eggs, sugar, flour and almonds, made according to a very ancient recipe.

Torta alla senese – Cake made with rice, milk, eggs, raisins and dried fruit, flavousred with lemon.

Torta de' Medici – Formed of two disks of pie dough filled with a mixture of spinach, Tuscan mustard, sugar, candied oranges, eggs, raisins, macaroons, flour, dried fruit and spices. In the past it was filled with a mixture of honey, cooked apples, spinach, and almonds and covered with a crust made of bread dough.

Zuppa del Duca – Created in the 16th-17th century in honour of the Duke of Correggio or perhaps of Grand Duke Cosimo III de' Medici, this sweet – made of cream and ladyfingers dipped in Alkermes – is the first version of the more famous one that, brought to Florence, was renamed "zuppa inglese" (English pudding) because it was so popular among the British residing there.

INDEX OF SIGHTS